"O Grefft i Gryfder"

(From Skill to Strength)

The COLEG LLANDRILLO CYMRU Story

by

Gillian Evans, BA (Hons), CIPFA

nereus

"O Grefft i Gryfder"
(From Skill to Strength)
The COLEG LLANDRILLO CYMRU Story

by Gillian Evans, BA (Hons), CIPFA

Limited Edition: September 2011

ISBN 978-0-9563229-3-7

Commissioned by
Coleg Llandrillo Cymru

Designed and published
by nereus, Tanyfron, 105 High Street,
Bala, Gwynedd, North Wales, LL23 7AE
Tel: (01678) 521229 e-mail: dylannereus@aol.com

Printed by Cambrian Printers,
Llanbadarn Fawr, Aberystwyth SY23 3TN
Tel: 01970 613000 www.cambrian-printers.co.uk

FOREWORD

St Trillo's dedicated chapel, as many dating from the 'Age of Saints', apparently boasted a continuously-flowing well, providing an endless supply of water for baptism. Reading this living history of the institution that today carries the name of Llandrillo throughout Wales and beyond, we can only take pride in the breadth and depth of the flow of educational and training provision it has provided for more than a century. Here is a story of determined development and growth of provision, focused initially on local student need, but aiming always for the highest national and international standards.

It is an inspiring story read from the perspective of today's achievements, but in reading it we are continually reminded how similar are the challenges faced from decade to decade. A lack of clarity about the legal and administrative framework of UK and Wales's national governance and funding of institutions, together with conflicting definitions of needs and requirements, was matched only by conflicts of local governance and provision, exacerbated by small-scale local government structures, and matching mentalities. A deep concern about the skills need of the North Wales's regional economy could often be deflected by definitions of the form of intended provision: was it technical or vocational, craft or trade, adult or liberal, business-oriented or citizenship-driven.

In each decade – and much longer for a very special few – we can recognise those key figures that provided leadership capable of taking advantage of opportunities and crises to focus on the need for change. Some were business leaders from the always significant hotel and catering industry of Llandudno, or experienced directors of commercial and manufacturing companies. Others were gifted dedicated teachers and trainers able to inspire students of all ages and achievement to transform themselves, and consequently their communities' prospects. A rarer breed were the imaginative administrators of education policies and services, determined, as one wrote, to build on the interests of pupils, both in vocational and cultural subjects 'in the development of the cultured citizen'. Since the heady post-war days of those words, the dreamed of 'county college' has under a long inspiring leadership become a leading nationally-funded institution, as Coleg Llandrillo Cymru has rightly boasted by its name and presence across North Wales and beyond.

In the second decade of the 21st century the aspirations of thirty or more learning pathways are being realised for all post-16 students across Welsh institutions, with Llandrillo a natural main provider. With a thinning red line between further and higher education being further rubbed out by worked-through genuine partnerships, a range of student and regional needs are capable of being met by real choice of provision, with an easier progression of qualification. That this extends from Llŷn on the western coast and beyond another Llandrillo to the east is a vision realised. Not quite that of the age of saints, but undoubtedly a more secular 21st century equivalent.

Dafydd Elis Thomas

Acknowledgements

Over the last eighteen months this book seems to have dominated my life. It has challenged me enormously to create a manuscript that not only fulfils the requirements of my commission from the Board of Coleg Llandrillo Cymru but is of a sufficiently high standard to meet the expectation of my readers. In this respect, I owe a great deal to Dylan Nereus who has guided me with the design and supported the very many changes I have made prior to publishing.

It would also be remiss of me to say this is all my own work. From start to finish, I have called upon people continually to offer me that fresh piece of information or photograph which adds to the chronological order of events that have occurred. We began way back in January 2010, with a personal invitation to a group of former staff and students who we knew had connections with the Technical Institute or the Hotel & Catering School. This meeting was to prove invaluable as it unearthed some very deep memories of former times which steered the research and opened the investigations. I am therefore indebted to Ellen Roberts (née Hughes), Doris Turton, Len Maddocks, David Williams, John Hughes, Haydn Thomas, Len Ellis, Mr and Mrs H.W. Edmondson and Mr T.I.G. Barrasford for getting me started. To these I must add Brenda Cox and Peter Deacon for our meetings and the supply of old photographs from the Hotel & Catering School, Ron Jones, former Project Architect of Llandrillo Technical College, for all his old newspaper reports and 'green site' photographs, Brian Whittingham for an old Technical Institute prospectus and Margaret Williams (née Roberts) for her memories.

Left to right:
Jane Cater
Toby Prosser
Anona (Non) Sampson

I was also fortunate to have a strong team around me: Toby Prosser, Jane Cater and Anona (Non) Sampson. Having direct access to College staff has been invaluable – Toby, Clerk to the Corporation, for his long-standing support with the photographs and links with the Board; Jane, Publications & Events Manager, for her beneficial critical review of the manuscript prior to design; and Non, the Principal's Personal Assistant, for her patience and endurance along each step of the way.

I must also thank Nick Hill and Andrew Mercer from the Marketing Department for their support with finding photographs, Lesley Ward from the College Library for bringing to our attention the College 'scrap books', Richard Turner for information about his father Tony Turner and Brian Swindells for his help with the sequencing of the accommodation changes.

A big thank you also to College staff, past and present, who have responded to my persistent requests for information and photographs: Mike Evans, Shyam Patiar, Pauline Dale, Gerry Jenson, Celia Jones, Julia Hughes, Mary Pritchard, Louise Jowett, Jackie Doodson, Melanie Montieth, Barbara Eden, Bob Gleave and Sheila Jones.

I would also like to thank Denbighshire Archives Services for copies of the minutes of the CBETCC and D. WhitesideThomas, Researcher at Gwynedd Archives, Museums & Arts Service for unearthing many of the older documents relating to the Hotel & Catering School. I must also thank David Roberts, Registrar of Bangor University, for his review of the manuscript and his time and support throughout and Lord Dafydd Elis Thomas for agreeing to write the Foreword.

And finally a very big thank you to Huw, my husband, and Sarah, my daughter, who have enthusiastically helped and supported me despite their own work and study commitments.

Gillian Evans

Photographs, Pictures and Illustrations

The majority of photographs and pictures in this book are drawn from sources within the College. Some, however, originate from private collections and, where known, their use is gratefully acknowledged below:

Mr John Lawson Reay, Photographer and Historian, Llandudno—for a variety of the College opening shots (1965) and Paynes Café pictures.
The late "Ricki" (Joeffre Cull), of Colwyn Studios—1960's Open Days; selection of Barberry Hill pictures.
Mr Mervyn Wynne Jones, Tremeirchion, from the archive of the late Ivor Wynne Jones, and by kind permission of Landmark Publishing Ltd.—Picture of Argyle Road Nisson Huts.
Raphael Tuck & Sons Limited—Vintage picture of Rhos Abbey Hotel attributed to "The Worlds Art Service".
The Daily Post and the **North Wales Weekly News** newspapers—for various cuttings.
Sean Gallagher, Commercial Photography, Cottingham—Cover aerial images.

PREFACE

From a modest beginning in Colwyn Bay, Coleg Llandrillo Cymru has grown to be one of the largest colleges in Wales and one of the most successful in the UK. Its operations now extend over the counties of Conwy, Denbighshire and more recently a significant part of Gwynedd. Students are attracted from across the region and increasingly include a vibrant international dimension.

When the Board decided to commission this work, it did so in the knowledge that no complete record existed of the history, growth and development of the College. This seemed to many of us a serious omission as the College had played such an important part in the lives of local people and the infrastructure of the area. The College is indebted to the work of the author, Gill Evans, who has carefully gathered evidence from previously unseen records, charting a story which reflects the evolution of the College, set within the Further Education sector in Wales. This is placed within a local context which provides an insight into the changing socio-economics of the North Wales coast and the demands on education and training.

The strength of the College is its staff that have helped shape the institution and helped it adapt to the demands of a changing world. I am privileged to be one of only three Principals who have led the College since its inception, each one uniquely responding to the challenges of the day.

The College focus is also one of skills development, which has been complemented by a rigorous approach to academic study. The College has constantly demonstrated innovation whilst embracing change and I can think of no more appropriate title for the book than 'O Grefft i Gryfder' – 'From Skill to Strength' – which was to become the motto of the Institute sometime around 1957.

As I write, the College has completed the most recent phase of its development involving the merger with Coleg Meirion-Dwyfor. This is seen as an integral part of the 'Transformation' process in Wales, which will result in larger, more strategic institutions. It is pleasing to note that the College is once again taking the lead in this change.

This book celebrates a story of expansion and development, of modernisation and of an institution finding its place within its community. It is indeed a tribute to the College that most of the people you meet from the area have, at some point, been involved with the College either as a student, a member of staff, a supplier of goods or services or indeed all three!

The College, over the years, has touched the lives of many people so I do hope you enjoy reading this account of the challenges, successes and themes which have shaped the history of what is today, Coleg Llandrillo Cymru.

Huw Evans, OBE, Principal 1989 to 2011

Author's Introduction

It is hard to believe that the first recordings of further education in the west of the old county of Denbighshire can be traced back to the year 1905. From these humble beginnings at the turn of the twentieth century, further education flourished, and so developed one of the largest and most successful Colleges in the United Kingdom – Coleg Llandrillo Cymru.

This record charts the origins and history of this large North Wales College, concluding with its merger with Coleg Meirion-Dwyfor in 2010 to form a greatly enlarged and enhanced Coleg Llandrillo Cymru covering the county areas of Conwy, Denbighshire and Gwynedd.

We start our historical journey in Colwyn Bay in 1905 with just a handful of adult evening classes. By 1954, with the help of the Colwyn Bay Evening Technical Classes Committee, this provision had grown sufficiently to justify the creation of a Technical Institute in Colwyn Bay which provided a range of full-time and part-time classes to almost 1,000 students. Almost simultaneously, a smaller but significant development was taking place over the county boundary in Caernarvonshire. In 1952, the prestigious Llandudno Catering Centre, which was to become the Llandudno School of Hotel and Catering, opened its doors to provide full-time education to 30 students.

In 1964, these two impressive but significantly differently sized institutions came together to form Llandrillo Technical College with a student base of some 1,700 students. This new College was certainly a challenge: a joint venture between two neighbouring councils, the then Denbighshire and Caernarvonshire County Councils. Situated on the boundary of the two counties, the two County Councils collaborated to build this brand new college to serve the needs of the students from both West Denbighshire and East Caernarvonshire.

In 1992, with the Further & Higher Education Act, Llandrillo Technical College became independent and known as Llandrillo College. In 2001, following a new logo and re-branding, it changed to the name by which we know it today – Coleg Llandrillo Cymru.

For most of this history, I have drawn extensively on official and original sources of documentation to record a chronological order of events. However, it is the human memory that often recollects the missed disclosure and for this, I am very grateful to those who took time to complete research questionnaires or sit with me and remember.

I have also learned that no history record can ever be complete or inclusive of each and every person or event, but it is hoped that this interpretation of the events that form the historic trail of Coleg Llandrillo Cymru not only records the changes of significance that have taken place, but adds to the record some of those treasured memories that are part of the institution's development over time.

Success is owned by all and the College is proud of the fact that each and every member of staff has and continues to give the professionalism, the energy and the enthusiasm to keep the College at the forefront of developments.

Gillian Evans
September 2011

CONTENTS

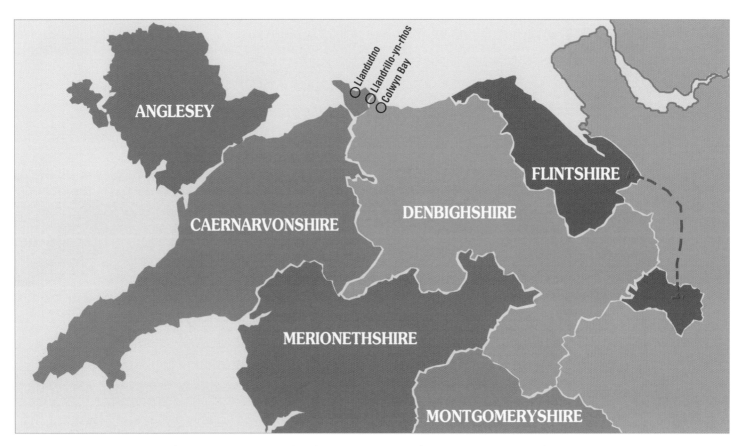

Map showing the old counties of North Wales prior to the 1972 reorganisation of local government boundaries.

1. Beginnings

The Early History of Technical Education

The county border sign just outside the College entrance.

By the end of the nineteenth century a variety of differently funded forms of continuing education was available. It included day-release, evening schools, mechanics institutes, schools of art, university extension lectures, tutorial classes and various forms of working men's colleges and courses.

At this time, concerns were constantly being expressed about the country's failing industrial performance, the inadequate state of education, including technical instruction, and the resulting weak educational background of the workforce which reduced international competitiveness.

These political concerns led to the Technical Instruction Act 1889, which permitted and provided funding for the newly formed local authorities to establish Technical Instruction Committees and levy rates to aid technical or manual instruction. However, 'Technical Education' was narrowly defined as 'instruction in the principles of science as applied to industries or employment, but not to the teaching or practice of any trade or industry'. The teaching of trade or craft processes was therefore excluded.

Amusingly, additional funds were provided by the Local Taxation (Customs and Excise) Act 1890, which diverted 'whisky money' away from publicans to local authorities to assist in either supporting technical education or relieving rates.

A new Education Act in 1902, drafted by A.J. Balfour (who later became Prime Minister), radically reorganised the administration of education at local level in England and Wales. The 1902 Act abolished the 2,568 school boards set up by the Elementary Education Act 1870, as well as all existing School Attendance Committees. Their duties were handed over to the local Borough or County Councils, using newly created Local Education Authorities (LEAs).

As well as continuing the functions previously performed by the school boards and the Technical Instruction Committees, the 328 new LEAs were all given powers to establish new secondary and technical schools. The abolition of the former school boards meant that the LEAs had to develop totally new systems and structures to manage their new responsibilities, which included paying for teachers, ensuring the teachers were properly qualified and providing necessary books and equipment. As a result, LEAs did not have the time, energy or resources to expand education generally.

The 1904 Secondary Schools Regulations continued the reforms and introduced a subject-based curriculum which included Drawing, English Language, Geography, History, Mathematics and Science as well as provision for manual work and physical education. Science instruction was to be both theoretical and practical.

As a result, at the start of the 20th Century, education in the College's immediate catchment area was the responsibility of three local authorities: the then Denbighshire County Council, its neighbour, Caernarvonshire County Council and the Borough of Colwyn Bay.

In 1905, with no designated College of Further Education/Technical School in the area, the Borough of Colwyn Bay established a wide range of adult education evening courses locally, including two vocational subjects: shorthand and typing. Initially, courses were held at the Board School in Douglas Road but in 1920, a rapid increase in student enrolments necessitated a move to the Higher Grade School at Dingle Hill (later known as Colwyn Bay Grammar School).

To cope with this rise in demand, the newly created Denbighshire County Council appointed a new Committee to manage adult education: The Colwyn Bay Evening Technical Classes Committee.

So from those early enrolments in 1905, the foundation stones of Coleg Llandrillo Cymru were laid.

Colwyn Bay Evening Technical Classes Committee

With the appointment in 1920 of the Colwyn Bay Evening Technical Classes Committee (CBETCC) and a full-time Supervisor, Mr F.C. Hobbs, to coordinate all adult education, enrolments in the area grew. Afternoon courses in women's crafts and domestic subjects (art, commerce and needlework) played a prominent part in the curriculum, as did engineering, building and science in the evening.

Colleges evolved slowly during the first half of the twentieth century, with many created from these early developments, including Mechanics' Institutions and Workingmen's Colleges. They were dependent on the support and insight of the newly created local authorities. Too often, the colleges had to operate in outmoded accommodation with outdated and inappropriate equipment, summed up by the expression 'make do and mend', a not unfamiliar phrase in further education until Incorporation in 1993.

Despite there being no defined college in the immediate vicinity, continuing education flourished within the Colwyn Bay area. Handwritten and bound minutes of the CBETCC (which was directly responsible to the Denbighshire Education Authority) from December 1937 until March 1954 reveal regular quarterly meetings which continued throughout the war. The net budget in 1938/39 was £900, of which £185 was raised through tuition fees. By July 1938, the range of provision was extensive: shorthand, art/needlework, dressmaking, cookery, Welsh, French, German, woodwork, plumbing, sciences, motor vehicle, electricity and telephony.

By 1939, further education enrolments had increased to over 1,000. This growth was in sharp contrast to many regions in England and Wales, where lack of funding following the First World War meant that only a few, forward-thinking local authorities had continued to develop adult provision, predominantly during the evening period. Enrolments continued to rise through the war years, mainly because of the large number of civil service staff and evacuees who relocated to the area as part of the war effort.

The Ministry of Food (MOF), created to oversee the production and distribution of food at the outbreak of war, relocated to Colwyn Bay in 1940. It commandeered many government buildings and hotels in the area to provide offices for its staff and canteens for the general public. The impact on the town was extensive; by 1942, an estimated 5,000 MOF staff and their families were living in or around Colwyn Bay and actively participating in local life. Penrhos School, which was occupied by the MOF during the war years, became a centre for many classes provided by the CBETCC, including speed shorthand, first aid and German.

With many children evacuated from Liverpool to the area too, the local population swelled and the demand for lodgings, schools and social activities increased. First hand reports from the time show relocation at all levels: schools became offices, hotels became schools, all to accommodate the instant growth in

				£	s	d
Salaries of Teachers				653	0	0
Books – Apparatus				150	0	0
Cleaning				40	0	0
Fuel – Light				90	0	0
Salary of Secretary				52	0	0
Printing – Advertising				80	0	0
Examination Expenses				6	13	6
Teachers' Travelling				5	0	0
Expenses of Exhibition				5	0	0
Supervisors' fee				50	0	0
				1131	13	6
Less Students fees	185	0	0			
Sale of Materials	1	0	0			
Cooking Sales	17	0	0			
Bank Interest	1	0	0			
Cr. Balance 1/9/38	27	13	6	231	13	6
Estimated Grant required from L.E.A.				900	13	6

The budget for 1938/39 as discussed at the meeting of the CBETCC on 27th September 1938.

Extracts from the minutes of the CBETCC on 2nd October 1939 (above and below).

population. For almost a decade, Colwyn Bay grew in prosperity and areas of the town flourished, including adult education.

Although the blackout brought its own challenges, it did not halt the demand for classes, which continued throughout the war years with reduced duration to 2.5 hours instead of 3 hours. Blackout curtains had to be purchased and it is recorded that the needlework classes, under the direction of Miss J.O. Douglas, were charged with making the curtains for the buildings occupied by the evening classes. This same part-time teacher not only transferred to the Technical Institute, Barberry Hill in 1954, but also went on to transfer to Llandrillo Technical College in 1964, before retiring in 1973. The CBETCC minutes also record that the cost of the blackout was to be spread to all that used the buildings, including the Liverpool Girls School that had evacuated to Colwyn Bay.

Space was always at a premium and the Committee were in constant dialogue with the Denbighshire County Architect to acquire new buildings. In 1939, the Committee looked at renting Bod Alaw, Rivieres Avenue – a three storey, semi-detached house near Colwyn Bay's town centre – for the painters, plumbers and upholsterers. By April 1943, the purchase of Bod Alaw meant the CBETCC had its first real home.

Before the classes could be opened, it was essential that the black out of the classrooms required should be completed and in this connection the following directions were submitted from the County Committee:
1. That curtain material and blue lamps should be procured by the County Architect in bulk and supplied to Schools and Evening Classes where required.
2. That School Managers and Evening School Committees be asked to submit measurements of windows of the rooms and particulars as to lights which will be required.
3. That the cutting of the curtain material and the sewing and hemming thereof be done by the Needlework Classes at the Schools and that Caretakers be asked to attend to the fittings.

As the war years were drawing to a close, the education system in England and Wales underwent a significant change. The Education Act 1944 introduced several major changes: free education to all pupils, the raising of the school leaving age to 15 (later to become 16) and a new tripartite system of education consisting of three types of secondary schools: grammar schools, secondary modern schools and secondary technical schools. All pupils were required to sit a national test (the 11+) to determine their eligibility to enter one of the three types of school.

The Act also provided for a review of further education by requiring each local authority to secure the provision of further education in their area through partnerships with other educational bodies e.g. universities, educational associations and the establishment of community colleges. Such colleges were to offer further education for young people who were not in full-time attendance at school which would include physical, practical and vocational training to develop and prepare them for the responsibilities of citizenship.

It was a difficult time for everyone. The aftermath of the war years left much to be done and, whilst the townsfolk were ready for their transient population returning to their home towns, the impact was deeper and faster than many had anticipated. Nearly one third of the MOF staff returned to London almost as quickly as they had arrived; others left over the next few years, the last few civil servants vacating the premises in Dinerth Road in 1956. Although the growth in adult education slowed as numbers in the town fell, the

'... Mr W. J. Griffiths, principal of Llandrillo College, chats with Miss J.O. Douglas of Colwyn Bay, who was retiring after teaching art, needlework and embroidery part-time for the Denbighshire Education Authority since 1937.'

A side view of the Barberry Hill residence showing the two huts at the rear of the house.

Council, the Ministry of Education and the Ministry of Labour supporting a potential development in the town.

In 1947, Bryn Eirias became a second contender for a Technical School, but there were complications arising from the lease on their buildings.

By 1948, the County Architect was in discussions to buy a private residence in Barberry Hill and in March 1949, the CBETCC made their first visit to the premises that were to become the home of adult education in the area. In April 1949, the CBETCC held the first of many meetings at Barberry Hill and most classes transferred from Bod Alaw to Barberry Hill in time for the academic session 1949/50.

In 1950, Bod Alaw became home to Ysgol Bod Alaw, a new home for primary age pupils in premises not entirely suited to the teaching of young children.

The early years of Barberry Hill were challenging. On the one hand, the CBETCC were told by Denbighshire

release of the Dinerth Road premises was later to prove an important consideration in adult education development in the western part of the county of Denbighshire.

In 1945, there is the first recorded entry of the proposed establishment of a Technical School in Colwyn Bay. Letters were sent by the CBETCC to Denbighshire County

Education Committee they had no jurisdiction in the running of Barberry Hill, yet in fact, many of the early decisions were managed by the CBETCC, such as those concerning the living accommodation for the full-time caretaker and the tenancy of the Poultry Keeper who resided in the grounds. Recorded in the minutes of the CBETCC in 1950 was a notice that an engineering workshop was to be erected in the grounds, with a second to follow. Two new permanent workshops followed to the rear of the house to accommodate engineering, carpentry and joinery, plumbing and gas fitting and motor vehicle.

In 1952, Denbighshire Education Committee formally recognised the demand for part-time, day-release courses in the west of the county and acknowledged that the younger people in the west faced considerable travel times to attend the new Technical College to the east in Wrexham. To rectify this issue and to provide a suitably qualified and locally available workforce for the emerging industries, plans were made to open Barberry Hill as the Authority's second Technical College.

In September 1952, the Director of Education stated that he wanted to develop the building as a full-time education centre; in November, a special committee was set up to develop the Colwyn Bay Technical Institute.

In 1953, the Housing Committee of Colwyn Borough Council was asked to permit a change of use from private residence to a Technical School. 'It was resolved that no objection be made to the change of use' (ref: minute 1004 Housing Committee, Colwyn Borough Council).

In September 1953, as preparations were being made to appoint a new Principal, Mr F.C. Hobbs retired after 33 years of devoted service to adult education.

2. The Technical Institute at Barberry Hill, Colwyn Bay

Mr W.J. Griffiths, BSc (Hons), Dip Ed., A.Inst.P

Prospectus of the Technical Institute, 1958/59.

In 1954, the new Technical Institute officially opened its doors. The newly appointed Principal, Mr W.J. Griffiths BSc, came to the Institute with a wide experience of teaching in the secondary and college sectors, plus the requisite discipline, having served during the war in the Royal Navy. A native of Cardiganshire, he was an honours graduate of University College, Aberystwyth. His task was simple: to expand the work of the Institute.

The new Technical Institute was formed to provide elementary technical courses in engineering and building, in addition to a full range of commercial courses. After successfully completing the technical courses at Colwyn Bay, students who wished to pursue more advanced courses could transfer to the then senior college at Wrexham. The greatest demand for courses was in automobile engineering, commerce, nursing and personal services, with hairdressing also becoming a major contender for the teaching space following a strong appeal from the trade.

Whilst a fundamental step in the right direction, Barberry Hill was almost immediately too small to meet student demand and largely inappropriate to meet the teaching needs expected.

From an examination of prospectuses, we learn that the Technical Institute continued to use premises around the area. By 1959, the decision was taken to rent a further 6,000 sq.ft. belonging to the vacating

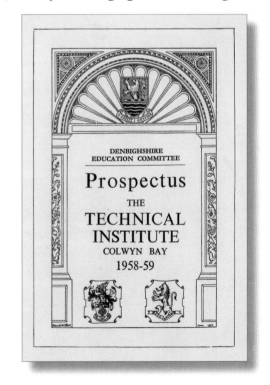

DENBIGHSHIRE
EDUCATION COMMITTEE

Prospectus

THE

TECHNICAL
INSTITUTE
COLWYN BAY
1958-59

Ministry of Food at Dinerth Road, bringing the total main teaching locations to eight. This later acquisition of space meant that Dinerth Road became the major provider of further education in the area.

The teaching locations in use between 1954 and 1960 were:

- Barberry Hill
- The annexe at Dinerth Road
- Pendorlan School and Colwyn Bay Grammar School for evening classes
- Bethlehem Church on Lawson Road for Painting and Decorating, Upholstery and Weaving
- Princess Street, Old Colwyn, for Brickworks
- Colwyn Bay Public Library for Librarianship courses
- A butcher's shop in Mochdre for Meat classes
- Typography classes at a printing works in Conwy

In essence, Barberry Hill remained structurally as a private residence and rooms were simply adapted to form 'plush'

'Consideration was given to the urgent necessity of obtaining accommodation for some vocational courses which are not established at the Institute owing to lack of accommodation. The Principal had obtained details of vacant premises which might prove suitable for accommodating Plastering, Bricklaying, Tiling, Painting and Decorating classes. Of these premises the following seemed most appropriate to meet the needs of the Authority:–

Bethlehem Church, Lawson Road, Colwyn Bay
Meredith & Kirkham Garage, Back of Princess Street, Old Colwyn.

… It was also resolved that … the time was now appropriate to make plans for the creation of a new block of buildings in the grounds of Barberry Hill consisting of classrooms, craftrooms, workshops, drawing offices and laboratories.'

teaching spaces and a dining room. The staff allocation of space was two small rooms – one for the Principal and the other for the administrative staff located at the top of the large sweeping stairway. There were no staff toilets or cloakroom and insufficient toilets for students.

Access to the premises was by way of a long twisting driveway which was surrounded by extremely well maintained lawns and borders. It is therefore no

Extract from the Governors' meeting held on 22nd December 1954.

A practical class for the metalwork students.

surprise to read that the issue of rabbit infestation within the grounds was regarded as a very serious matter; in July 1959, the Pest Officer of the Ministry of Agriculture and Fisheries was charged with the task of eradicating the pest!

A car parking area had been located at the front of the house, directly facing a steep embankment which descended to a small stream. Staff recall that on more than one occasion, visiting cars skidded on the surface and descended down the embankment, only to be rescued by the eager youngsters of the Motor Vehicle Department practising their vehicle recovery skills!

The Industrial Context

Prior to the Second World War, the Institute's catchment area was traditionally dominated by the Tourism Industry. The area boasted many large hotels that were focal points within the town for employment opportunities. However, at the outset of the Second World War, the re-locating Ministry of Food commandeered many of the hotels to support the war effort. This meant they could no longer attract visitors, even had the trade been there. Whilst the local economy flourished with the influx of civil servants and evacuees, it was clear that many hotels would never recover when the war was over. It is within this backdrop of change and a declining tourist trade that the plans for the new Institute took shape.

The years of war meant that most building maintenance programmes, both private and public, had been deferred and buildings now required significant maintenance and refurbishment. The hotels were no exception, having been used intensively to support the re-located schools, offices and troops.

Whilst it is not the intention to discuss the many changes resulting from the war that impacted upon education, the post-war years did present many challenges, including the need to feed and house a nation damaged by war. Such matters required immediate attention and had a major impact on many aspects of local day to day life, including education.

Colwyn Bay Borough Council was not complacent and immediately set about bringing change. There were many issues to tackle and, whilst initially trying to salvage some of the tourist attractions of old, they recognised that the future lay elsewhere. Faced with the demand for new housing, new roads for a greater numbers of cars, damaged sea defences and the need to take the town forward, ambitious plans were drawn up to create hundreds of new

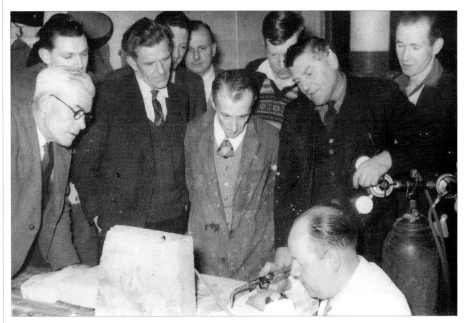

Employees on day-release programmes in Engineering.

dwellings, improve road networks, repair a significant stretch of the sea wall and create new job opportunities in light engineering.

Whilst already facing increasing demands from the construction and engineering trades, the emerging Institute took full advantage of all the new opportunities and developed courses to meet demands as they arose.

A presentation made during the College Open Day by members of the Governing Body.

Governance at the Technical Institute

Administratively, the Institute was managed by its own Governing Body. The twenty four members included fourteen members of the Denbighshire Education Committee, seven representatives from industry and commerce, one member of Colwyn Bay Borough Council and two co-opted members. In attendance were the Principal, the Director of Education and the Further Education Officer. The Governing Body, chaired by Alderman F.H. Andleby Jones throughout its existence, met every two months and detailed minutes record the challenges of managing this exciting new Institution.

The first industrial site in the area was located at Mochdre in 1957. The intention was to encourage local firms to relocate and provide all-year-round jobs for the townspeople in modern factory accommodation. Two such firms were internationally acclaimed: Quinton Hazell made spare parts for motor vehicles and J.K. Smit & Sons made diamond tools for mineral excavation. Both firms often required bespoke training from the Institute.

There were also nine Advisory Committees representing Building, Painting & Decorating, Engineering, Motor Vehicle, Electrical Installation, Commerce, Typography, Librarianship and Hairdressing. In their Inspection of 1960, the Inspectorate felt that there were too many Advisory Committees, partly because many represented a very small cohort of students, but also because the Principal was required to attend each and take the minutes. This fact is borne out when student numbers are analysed below, but was defended by the Principal who stated: '... *employers become impatient of generalities and platitudes which are commonplace in meetings of a more general nature.*'

Student Enrolments

From 1954 to 1960, the Institute's annual statistical record (Form 3 F.E.) shows a similar number of enrolments each year and, whilst there was concern about potential duplication of numbers between the day time and the evening, it is clear that the pattern of growth was changing: a move away from traditional evening classes to increasing numbers of part-time day students and full-time students. Further analysis of the enrolments shows that students from Llandudno and Conwy did attend the Institute, despite the statutory obligation for out-of-county students to attend the Bangor Technical College in Caernarvonshire. It has therefore been difficult to find completely accurate records of student enrolments across the

Logo of the Technical Institute, introduced sometime after 1957.

Student numbers derived from the statistical record Form 3 F.E.

The Technical Institute, Colwyn Bay

Student numbers shown on Form 3 F.E.

Year	Full Time	Part time Day	Part time Evening	TOTAL
1953/54	11	17	961	989
1954/55	29	71	1097	1197
1955/56	42	110	1000	1152
1956/57	44	229	969	1242
1957/58	56	104	960	1120
1958/59	86	218	678	982
1959/60*	131	313	776	1220

where* denotes Inspection figures in February 1960

Geographical location of students in 1959/60

	Colwyn Bay	Rest of Denbighshire	Caernarfonshire	TOTAL
Full Time	36	49	46	131
Part time Day - voc	92	37	70	199
Part time Day - non voc	92	13	9	114
Evening - voc	199	52	109	360
Evening - non voc	320	25	71	416

Student enrolments in 1959/60 (students have more than one entry)

Full Time Courses		Part time Day (vocational)		Part Time Day (non vocational)	
Commerce 1st year	24	Engineering etc	92	Civil Service	14
Commerce 2nd year	20	Telecomms	30	Crafts	110
Commerce post G.C.E	20	Commerce	18		
Pre-nursing 1st year	18	Hairdressing	30		
Pre-nursing 2nd year	12	Meat	8		
Pre-apprenticeship	13	Agriculture	6		
G.C.E	6	GCE 'O'	67		
Hairdressing 1st year	18	Librarianship	9		
TOTAL	131	TOTAL	260	TOTAL	124

Evening (vocational)		Evening (non vocational)	
GCE'O'	103	Languages	120
Engineering etc	155	Woodwork	39
Commerce	166	Art	33
Breadmaking	12	Crafts	228
Horticulture	13		
Librarianship	8		
TOTAL	457	TOTAL	420

Commerce students busy at Barberry Hill.

Hairdressing students at the Dinerth Road annexe.

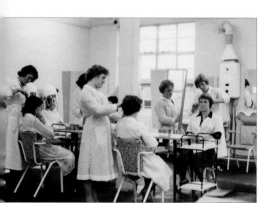

different programme areas as the registers held at the Institute clearly contained duplicate enrolments. This was common practice as many groups of students were mixed with other groups when space was limited and numbers were small. Despite such duplication, it has been possible to summarise course registration in sufficient detail to present the mix of student enrolments in the Institute at the time of the HMI Inspection in February 1960.

From the detail provided, the pattern of enrolment was as follows:

Commerce—the single largest department with a Head of Department responsible for a wide range of full and part-time provision.

Pre-Nursing—essentially a full-time vocational course developed in 1955 which recruited 15+ year old students from secondary schools.

Hairdressing—a full-time course which started in 1959 and part-time day-release courses, all housed in new and purposely adapted accommodation at Dinerth Road.

Engineering, Motor Vehicle & Building—included a full-time pre–apprenticeship course for secondary school leavers and a range of part-time day and evening courses at the Institute and other venues across the county area.

English & Liberal studies, Mathematics & Science—a range of provision essentially provided for full-time students but included GCE O level courses.

Radio & Telecommunications—part-time day-release courses essentially for employees of the Post Office Engineering Department.

Agriculture & Horticulture—part-time courses taught by members of the then Llysfasi Farm Institute who had established an outpost initially in Abergele and then latterly at the Institute.

Food subjects—one part-time day-release meat course and an evening bread making course held in the secondary school.

Librarianship—a part-time day course and an evening course.

Craft classes for Women—an extensive range of all aspects of needlework held at Barberry Hill and the secondary school.

Art classes—a range of art classes taught by a local teacher from the secondary school primarily for school children.

Across this range of provision were several courses specifically designed for different groups of employed students usually targeted at post-GCE standard, for example, on duty Fire Service employees during the day (with their fire engine on standby in the driveway), civil servants employed across a range of different departments and local police cadets. The educational needs of these students were quite diverse, both as regards subjects and intellectual attainment, which meant that conventional study was often wholly inappropriate.

In the case of the civil servants, enrolment took place throughout the year. In the absence of a 'modularised' curriculum, lecturing staff were often faced with a varying number of students who were attending simply because it was a condition of their employment. To accommodate such fluctuations in numbers and meet class size requirements, employed students were often mixed with classes of young full-time students which essentially changed the vocational nature of the education, as required by the employer. Needless to say this provision came under close scrutiny from the Inspectorate who were keen to see new course development using 'terminal' blocks

Students enjoying a lesson in handicrafts.

of study to improve content and variety. Modularisation was about to begin.

The changing nature of modes of attendance brought even greater challenges for the Institute. The already restricted accommodation and equipment became barely sufficient for the students attending. A shortfall also developed in the number of trained teaching staff available to teach the increasing number of students. Additional staff were gradually recruited to teach physical education and health/hygiene, economics and law, history and geography, art, science and handicrafts. Further shortages occurred with the number of teaching support staff and in particular the administrative office where staff were needed to implement a new student record system capable of recording the changing and varying types of enrolment.

Student Facilities

Prior to 1959 and the rental of major teaching space at Dinerth Road, full-time students were provided with a meal brought in containers from the School Meals Service in the dining room at Barberry Hill. Cups of tea could also be purchased and for many part-time students, this was the extent of the refreshments available. The situation worsened when some students transferred to Dinerth Road; the dining area was immediately put to other uses and the remaining students were left with no refreshment facilities at all. Former students state that lunches were either sandwiches brought from home or

A technical drawing class at Barberry Hill.

purchases made in local shops, with cups of tea made using kettles within their own teaching area. The lunch time rules were simple: ensure you were back on time or the door would be closed. For the full-time students, who relocated to Dinerth Road, things improved: lunch in the canteen or sandwiches in the classroom.

The growth in the number of full-time students not only created problems with refreshments. Many of the youngsters, aged just 15, were travelling long distances to attend their courses. The hairdressers, for example, were all young females attending the only provision in North Wales. It is recorded that the first intake of hairdressing students drew from no less than six county areas across North Wales. Lodgings and living away from home therefore became important factors for some, while those whose parents were unhappy with this option had no alternative but to travel excessive distances each day to attend their course of choice. Unsurprisingly, the Inspectors commented on this situation: *'It is hoped that eventually suitable hostel accommodation will be provided.'*

A group of students pose for the camera.

Student clubs and societies were difficult to organise within the Institute premises, but attempts were made to create evening social meetings once provision transferred to Dinerth Road. The Science laboratory initially earmarked for social meetings was not deemed suitable for social gatherings of excitable students! Undeterred, the students continued to organise an annual dance at the end of the summer term and enjoy the annual prize-giving at the Victoria Pier in Colwyn Bay, despite the fact that a new communal room was not provided until

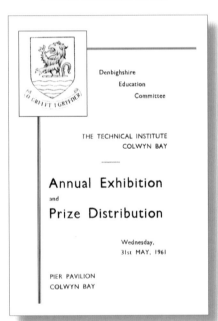

1961. The annual exhibition and prize-giving event at the Victoria Pier was a major event in the calendar of Colwyn Bay and the surrounding area. The exhibition with representations from most areas of the Institute, was formally opened to the public after lunch and was followed by the prize-giving ceremony in the evening. The event attracted many of the town's senior figures and is remembered with fondness and humour, including:

• The administration staff typing to music and awaiting the shout of *'carriage return'* before moving on to the next line of the music – all done to allow the sound of the carriages returning to co-incide with the music chosen;
• The painters and decorators painting the Borough coat of arms in competition for a prize;
• Cookery demonstrations including *flambé* cooking, with the public eager to taste, notwithstanding the improvisation of liquor that sometimes took place;
• Old vehicles for demonstration purposes that generously left their deposits of oil on the Pier surfaces.

It is recorded that by 1961, the Institute had established a Camera Club and a new Choral Party had been formed, following the purchase of a piano by the Institute.

Students also benefited from a wide range of demonstrations and competitions, both locally and further afield. Invitations were issued regularly by external organisations and employers for students from all curriculum areas to attend lectures, films and related subject demonstrations.

In 1961, the Institute supported the Commonwealth Technical Training Week, a national initiative which included national and local events. With all aspects of education and industry involved, the Institute played a major role in the week-long events, staged primarily in Colwyn Bay Town Hall. This included a mid-week Open Day and prize-giving, a careers convention, a young persons' dance on Thursday evening and a Concert on Friday morning with members of the Friendship Club.

In contrast, and a major shortcoming during the life of the Institute, student physical education was undoubtedly limited. There were opportunities to play tennis on locally rented courts for students with the necessary equipment, and an evening class in Keep Fit was available for some students. For those who enjoyed swimming, arrangements had been made at the local pool at a concessionary rate. Generally, there was consensus that the lack of facilities for physical education was a serious deficiency, but until the availability of suitable accommodation or playing fields became available, the matter was to be deferred.

In January 1962, following the creation of a student communal room, members of the Institute Film Society released the first College magazine. A handwritten black and white publication priced 6d, the 'Screen', became an energetic means of advertising within the student community. Common features included student experiences, forthcoming films at the local cinemas and the top 20 hits, where Cliff Richard and Elvis Presley featured consistently. It is also recorded that in May 1962, the long awaited movie on College Life was released with final showings taking place that same month. No trace has been found of this movie at the time of writing!

It is worthy of mention that sometime in 1961, a decision was taken to change the name of the Technical Institute to the Technical College. The prospectus for 1961/62 promotes the Technical College whilst the brochure for the Annual Exhibition of May 1961 retains the name as Technical Institute. The first edition of 'Screen' in January 1962 refers to the Technical College and noticeably the minutes of the Governors, after February 1962, refer to the Technical College. No records have been found explaining why the change occurred although one might assume it resulted from the White Paper issued in 1961.

Issue No I
January 1962

MINISTRY OF EDUCATION
(WELSH DEPARTMENT)

REPORT BY H.M. INSPECTORS ON

Colwyn Bay Technical Institute,
Denbighshire

INSPECTED week beginning 1st FEBRUARY, 1960

NOTES

THIS REPORT is confidential and may not be published save
by the express direction of the competent authority of the
School. If published it must be included in its entirety.

The copyright of the Report is vested in the Controller of
H.M. Stationery Office. The Controller has no objection
to the reproduction of the Report provided that it is clearly
understood by all concerned in the reproduction that the
copyright is vested in him.

MINISTRY OF EDUCATION, (WELSH OFFICE),
8, CATHEDRAL ROAD, CARDIFF

W.T. 4/60

Report by HM Inspectors,
February 1960.

HM Inspectors' Report February 1960

In early 1960, an independent inspection of the Technical Institute was carried out. Despite the best efforts of this new and energetic Institute, its use of a range of premises to accommodate the many new courses developed over this short period of time did not meet with the same enthusiasm from the Inspectorate.

HM Inspectors reported that '... *the premises [Barberry Hill] have been adapted to provide four classrooms of 380, 192, 295 and 154 sq.ft., a laboratory of 380 sq.ft., a drawing office of 295 sq.ft., and a room for radio work of 250 sq.ft. ... at the rear of the house the prefabricated huts contain a Carpentry and Joinery workshop of 960 sq.ft., and an Engineering workshop of 1110 sq.ft. adjoining a Plumbing and Gas Fitting workshop of 540 sq.ft. ...'* They then went on to say ... *'the work of the College is thus carried on in eight different sets of premises situated between Old Colwyn, Mochdre and Rhos-on-sea. Much of the accommodation is of an improvised nature, sub standard in size,* which has been adapted for teaching purposes. *Some of the specialist rooms, such as workshops, are frequently in use for purposes for which they were not planned. Dressmaking has, for example, to be done in the carpentry and joinery shop or in small classrooms; heavy craft work is carried out in the painting and decorating room; specialist rooms are often in use for general teaching purposes.*

It would be pointless to describe in detail the many disadvantages and drawbacks arising from the present situation, since so many of the deficiencies in equipment also arise from inadequate premises, such as lack of storage space and the need for using the same piece of equipment, for example, visual and aural aids in rooms situated in different parts of the Borough.

There can be no adequate and final solution to the accommodation problem until the College is re-housed in new premises, and it is recommended that this should be done as soon as possible.'

As Mr Griffiths and his Governors had been tasked with expanding provision for students across the West of Denbighshire without the support of any new, purpose-built accommodation, they responded vigorously, defending their actions by reference to employers' demands and Ministry of Education circulars.

Many of the early shortcomings were actually being resolved with the additional space acquired in 1959 at Dinerth Road, although it is clear from the records of the Governors' meetings that not all issues could be resolved or improved without further additional funding. One particular casualty of the accommodation shortfall was Motor Vehicle, which had been confined to one small corner of the engineering workshop. Improvisation was always necessary and practical lessons using the vehicles stored outside were only made possible with hastily erected tarpaulin over adjoining wooden frames to protect the students from the rain.

Suffice to say, a new purpose-built technical college was the only acceptable solution but, as the minutes of meetings in 1959 confirm, planning for a new College of Further Education had already begun before the Inspectors arrived.

Both Denbighshire and Caernarvonshire had been under tremendous pressure to find new educational accommodation and, quite independently of each other, made application to the Ministry of Education to sanction new and appropriate buildings for their technical provision. As one might expect, the Ministry strongly advised the two

A carpentry class (above) and a dressmaking class (below) – the same room, but two very different uses.

local authorities to talk to each other and seek one alternative – a college in the Llandudno/Colwyn Bay area which would serve the needs of West Denbighshire and East Caernarvonshire.

In September 1959, representatives of both Denbighshire and Caernarvonshire met with officials of the Ministry of Education in London. On 6 October 1959, at a meeting convened at the Technical Institute between representatives of the two counties and the Inspectorate, it was reported that Sir David Eccles, the Minister of Education, had given approval in principle for the erection of a College of Further Education to serve the needs of the Colwyn Bay/Llandudno Area. It was also stated that the college should be erected as two separate buildings: one to house the Llandudno Hotel & Catering School, the other to house the College of Further Education. You will read more about the Hotel & Catering School in the next section.

The approval was granted on condition that a suitable site was found, which enabled both buildings to be erected in such close proximity that they could be easily intercommunicated. All the buildings were, however, to be under the supervision of one College Principal.

At the time, therefore, of the Technical Institute Inspection in 1960, discussions for a new college were well under way. Following HM Inspectors' Report in February 1960, the matter of a new college was firmly placed back with the County Architect's Department for a solution.

The minutes of the Governing Body meeting on 4 October 1960 record that a proposed new college, to become a joint college between the counties of Denbighshire and Caernarvonshire, was being considered and that the Governors of the Institute were to be given the opportunity to consider any future proposal prior to the Denbighshire Education Committee taking a final decision.

After the Inspection, robust assessments of teaching requirements, together with a thorough pruning of provision, resulted in a reduction in the number of premises in favour of renting further appropriate space at Dinerth Road. By 6 February 1961, the Director of Education reported that a number of recommendations contained in the report had been, or were in the process of being carried out. These included the transfer of painting and decorating to Barberry Hill and the centralisation of all Institute matters within the two centres – Barberry Hill and Dinerth Road. The additional space at Dinerth Road provided a new student communal room, a new library, needlework room, art room, science room and a female staff toilet and staff room. The issue of student lodgings was also being addressed, with an application being made to the Ministry of Education for a student hostel.

Matters of concern continued to appear on the Governors' meeting agendas. Even with the most efficient pruning and relocation of courses, some venues had to be retained to meet growing numbers of students in certain areas, e.g. the Brickwork shop tenancy.

In their report, the Inspectors had also analysed occupational areas over both the West Denbighshire and East Caernarvonshire regions despite the Institute being most firmly within Denbighshire. This effectively highlighted the importance of the Catering and Hotel trades and challenged the potential for course development within the Engineering and Building trades, where seemingly small numbers of students were involved, a factor that was to play a very contentious role in the future development of the new college.

Representation was made by the Institute reminding the Inspectorate that had they excluded the East Caernarvonshire statistics, the Engineering and Building trades could be shown to play a very significant part within the employment patterns in the locality – a matter strongly supported by the Colwyn Bay Labour Exchange.

It was also pointed out to the Inspectors that the Institute was working primarily with small and medium-sized employers who simply did not allow their employees to attend college during the day which materially affected recruitment at apprenticeship level. Consequently many courses had been run uneconomically over the early years of development which added to the challenges of accommodation type and future sustainability.

In January 1961, the Minister of Education presented the White Paper on 'Better Opportunities in Technical Education'. This paper was to have a major impact on course provision for technicians, craftsmen and operatives. The intention was clear:

- To improve and broaden education received by students, providing the maximum continuity between the education at school and technical college;
- To adapt the system more closely to the needs of industry;

A group of full-time students and staff of the Technical Institute, Colwyn Bay, 1961 (and on following pages).

- To increase and make better provision for technicians;
- To substantially reduce the waste which occurred through poor completion rates.

The Institute responded, quickly holding two meetings in January 1961 with the industrialists from the Building and the Engineering sectors. The meetings were designed not only to reassure the Institute that they were providing the correct type of courses which were adequately staffed but to explore future demands and seek the co-operation of the employers themselves. In general, the responses were positive and there was a consensus that the Institute and the industry should work together to increase the number of apprentices and

ensure that sufficient numbers were trained to meet the growing demand for the newer industries and the more nationally established industries like MANWEB.

For the Institute, this meant an increase in students attending during the day, improved selection criteria, the inclusion of national certificate and diploma courses, technical courses developed for particular industries, craft courses and courses for operatives. No student was to rely

wholly on evening study, which meant a much greater commitment from local employers with day-release, sandwich and block-release styles of provision being encouraged.

In many ways, this laid down the pattern of attendance for the coming years and began to shape the college as a responsive, outward-looking institution. The foundations for the future were beginning to be established.

3. The Llandudno School of Hotel and Catering

Llandudno Catering Centre

At the same time as the developments in education were gaining pace in Colwyn Bay, so too were developments in Llandudno. As the economy recovered from the war years, during which most hotels in the area had been requisitioned by some government department or other, the industry faced a significant challenge to restore the hotel

Charles Payne, Chairman of Llandudno Council chats to the students.

trade. The Hotel & Catering Institute in London decided that to rebuild its future, it needed to improve standards and training.

A rigorous campaign was launched from the Institute in London to persuade local education authorities to establish local educational and training facilities, either in separate schools or as new departments in technical colleges. Entry to the Institute would now require a recognised qualification from the London City & Guilds, a professional examining body that had been in existence for over a century. The campaign extended to North Wales when a group of prominent Llandudno hoteliers – including Messrs Eric Cox, Charles Payne and J. Town – approached the Director of Education.

Sometime in April 1949, the issue of technical education and the proposed County Colleges was discussed at length at a Caernarvonshire County Council meeting. The author of the report, Mr Mansell Williams, Director of Education reported the following: *'So much has been written and said about County Colleges that most of us have come to regard them almost as mythical fairy castles which will be erected here long after we have left.'*

All local authorities were waiting for the Ministerial order to establish the county colleges but in Caernarvonshire, the decision was taken to proceed to build upon the foundations that already existed. It was reported that students attending technical classes were on the increase; 46 students in 1948 rising to 153 by April 1949. Employers in the area had appreciated the limited facilities and had allowed their employees to be released for one day, without a loss of pay. As with the provision in Colwyn Bay, most classes were overcrowded and extra accommodation was urgently required.

Mansell Williams, however, showed considerable foresight when, in the body of his report, he drew attention to the false division between different branches of education: '... *it is an old established principle that the educator must build on the interests of his pupils... too often do we hear of vocational and cultural subjects referred to as if they were separate things; forgetting that we are dealing with single personalities in whom the vocational and cultural interests are unified... the county colleges will therefore assist in the development of the cultured citizen and its approach will be through the vocation of the pupils'.*

The conclusions were to develop county colleges which would specialise and offer examination courses related to a particular vocation. Students were to be required to sit examinations including the London City & Guilds and the Union of Lancashire and Cheshire Institutes. The proposals for the Caernarvonshire colleges included Llandudno Junction for catering or light engineering, Bangor for mechanical engineering and Botwnnog for agriculture. It was also stated that there was still a need for Coleg Harlech and the Workers' Educational Association classes after the county colleges had been established.

By June 1949, the proposals in catering were beginning to take shape. The Reconstruction Committee of Caernarvonshire County Council approved, in principle, the suggestion outlined by the Director, to establish facilities for catering instruction in some of the War Department huts acquired in Conway Road. This, however, was not the first catering instruction to be provided in Llandudno; several months later in September 1949, we learn that the Further Education

Committee received a report to say that a catering class had already been running for twelve months in Llandudno, with great success. At this same meeting, agreement was given to accommodate the class by adopting part of the buildings at Conway Road, alongside the recently located Welsh School. Plans were clearly advanced, as the HM Inspectors had already been consulted regarding the equipment required for the demonstration room at a cost of £1,000.

In October 1950, the Building Committee of the Caernarvonshire County Council reported that four tenders had been received for the Llandudno Catering Centre at the War Department huts. The contract, financed by way of loan, was awarded to a local Llandudno builder, Messrs John Owen, in the sum of £1,399 18s 0d.

In June 1951, the Technical Education Sub-Committee was given the power to appoint a Teacher-in-Charge and on 17th October 1951, following consideration of the applications, four candidates were placed on the short list. At the same meeting, the Committee also approved the fees to be charged to students attending the Centre, for review after twelve months:

A Nissan hut, similar to those used by the School of Hotel & Catering.

Student Fees		
Students under 18, on September 1st		
— 5/- per day of week per course		
Students over 18, on September 1st		
— £1 per day of week per course		
Students attending evening classes		
— 10/- per evening of week per course		

On 31st October 1951, with the Chairman and Secretary of the Catering Section of the Llandudno Chamber of Trade acting in an advisory capacity, Mr Francis E.

O'Mahoney from Aldershot was appointed to the post and awarded the maximum rate for Grade B Assistants under the Scale of Salaries for Teachers in Establishments for Further Education: £725 per annum.

By November 1951, a supplementary award of £200 was needed for the Catering Centre towards the cost of furniture, apparatus and equipment.

At a special meeting of the Technical Education Sub-Committee in April 1952, following an inspection by members of the committee, the future of the Catering Centre was discussed. It is evident from the decisions taken at the meeting that the costs of the Centre were continuing to increase. They included:

1. A loan of £1,600 to finance adaptations to buildings at a cost of £1,187 18s 0d and equipment at £412.
2. The appointment of a caretaker/kitchen cleaner and a storekeeper/clerk to commence duties from the opening of the Centre.

In addition, it was noted that equipment had been provided, on a free loan, by the Wales Gas Board to the value of £1,500 and the North Wales Electricity Board to the value of £479.

At the Technical Education Sub-Committee on 4th September 1952, the following rates of pay were approved for part-time lecturers at the Llandudno Catering Centre and the Bangor Technical Institute, placing them on an equal footing:

| Grade | Work of | Per Hour | |
		Men £	Women (⁴⁄₅ men's rate) £
I	Below S1 standard	10/6	8/6
II	S1 and S2 standards	13/6	11/-
III	S3 standard	15/6	12/6
IV	A1, A2 and upwards	17/6	14/-

In September 1952, the Llandudno Catering Centre opened to both full-time and part-time students in Llandudno. The first intake comprised seven students, five girls and two boys. Most were just 16 years old and all lived locally except one girl from

Mr Francis E. O'Mahoney, Teacher-in-charge.

Caernarfon, who was expected to reside in the area during the week and return home at weekends. This first intake recruited its students from advertisements placed in the *Caernarvon & Denbigh Herald*. None of the original seven were the children of local hoteliers, although this was to change significantly in future years.

Under the leadership of Mr F. O'Mahoney, the Centre proved to be an outstanding success despite the limitations in the accommodation. It is recorded that only 24-30 student places were available at the Centre, which is supported by a copy of a 'team' photograph. It is also known that despite limitations in size, the huts boasted a well-sourced kitchen area and a public café which enabled students to serve their culinary produce and practise their waiting-on skills to the public at lunchtime.

The School was also fortunate in attracting and retaining able and efficient staff. The three original staff, Messrs O'Mahoney, May and Whittington all remained throughout the early developments and transferred to the new Llandrillo Technical College in 1964 to form the nucleus of its new Catering Department.

In 1953, the success of the Centre was evident through the demands for more teaching staff. At the Education Committee

Students and Staff at the Centre in 1957.

Girls from the first intake of 1952 during the practical sessions.

Diners are made aware of the 'training' requirements.

CAERNARVONSHIRE EDUCATION COMMITTEE

Hotel and Catering School,
Conway Road,
LLANDUDNO.

Head of Department
F.E. O'Mahoney, M.H.C.I.

Dear Sir/Madam,

We are extremely pleased to welcome you to our School for Luncheon, and should like to thank you for the assistance and encouragement which you are in this way giving us.

It is only through your co-operation that we can attain high standards of courtesy and service. You may occasionally find the service a little slow, and you will undoubtedly notice that our movements do not display the ease and skill of the fully trained person. We are, however, at the moment only learning the trade and we hope that you will be patient and tolerant.

You may, if you wish, give gratuity, 30 per cent. of which will be devoted to Charity and 70 per cent. to our own Students' Amenities Fund.

We shall be pleased to hear your comments, which should be addressed to the Lecturer-in-Charge.

Yours faithfully,

Ranee Sumlu

Student Prefect.

in January 1953, a supplementary vote of £155 was approved to meet the cost of additional part-time teaching staff. The Centre also hosted its first annual dinner for prominent people connected with the North Wales catering industry. Over the years, these included the Prime Minister, Sir Anthony Eden in October 1956, Ministers of Education, Sir Edward Boyle and Mr Christopher Chataway.

The Llandudno School of Hotel & Catering, as it was to become known, was one of only a few places where students could obtain the five diplomas which comprised the entrance requirement both to higher education and to some of the highest paid posts in the sector. For many students, a move to the Birmingham College of Food or the Blackpool Technical College was necessary to progress their studies to Higher National Certificate (HNC) level. The School therefore attracted many students to the area and so the demand for lodging began.

A student's paradise – the Majestic Ballroom and Paynes Café in Llandudno.

There were clear links with the Caernarvonshire School Meals Service. Students recall that not only were their dinners supplied by the service, but also the formidable Mrs Pritchard who oversaw the quality of provision!

Education was not limited to catering subjects; students were required to study the utilities, typing and book-keeping, most of which took place in the dining area of the Nissan hut or the local Secondary Modern School. The students were also expected to work long hours and a mandatory part of their education was evening duties at the banquets held at the Imperial Hotel, where they received 7s 6d per night. The reward for such long hours was the annual trip out, usually to Hotel Olympia in London.

Recreational facilities were limited, although former students do remember the odd game of table tennis on the pastry table! Entertainment however was in their veins and the students energetically became the organisers of the dances at Payne's Café and Ballroom in Llandudno. Sometimes three or four events were held each year, dependent on sufficient numbers to pay the bills. Artistic skills also became a requirement for these young organisers as flyers were needed to attract their audiences, sometimes being distributed as far afield as the University in Bangor.

With the full support of the larger hotels, it soon became clear that larger, more appropriate accommodation was needed, not only to teach the students the range of subjects required, but also to provide the students with some communal facilities. As we have learned, in 1959 the Caernarvonshire County Council commenced talks with the Minister of Education and Denbighshire County Council to provide new and enhanced premises for the Llandudno School of Hotel & Catering and the Technical Institute in Colwyn Bay.

From the outset, the demand for quality and appropriate accommodation was clear. The schedule discussed at the meeting in 1959 included:

- An advanced kitchen
- A training kitchen
- A food demonstration kitchen
- A food science laboratory
- Patisserie
- Butchery larder
- Restaurant
- Dining room
- Hotel suite
- Home management laundry

… and much more!

Students enjoying the sunshine outside the front entrance.

4. Llandrillo Technical College – Foundations

The green field site chosen for the new Llandrillo Technical College.

Building Design

From the outset, the early discussions about the site of the new college related to land adjoining the border of the two counties. The Education Officer for Denbighshire hoped the college would be situated immediately to the west of Llandrillo Church and on the north side of the 'Colwyn Bay – Llandudno Road' in Denbighshire. The Education Officer for Caernarvonshire inspected a site on the south side of the 'Colwyn Bay – Llandudno Road' in Caernarvonshire but it was too marshy. Discussions also centred on the possibility of erecting the Catering School on a part of the nearby golf course in Caernarvonshire within a few yards of the Denbighshire/Caernarvonshire border.

In 1960, the site for a new Technical College at Llandrillo-yn-rhos was finally selected: on the boundary of the two counties, but with its foothold most firmly in Denbighshire. There was some dissent about the final location from a few Llandudno councillors, but overall there was overriding agreement that the general welfare of the young people was more important than civic pride. The development was to be a shared venture between the two County Councils, a factor that would be extremely important in the early years of the new college. Following considerable local debate, a name that reflected its location was finally agreed: Llandrillo Technical College.

Right from the start, as space for the new college was being determined, there was one contentious issue. In the Minister's view, which was possibly influenced by the

The site for the new college at Llandrillo-yn-rhos.

Inspection Report of 1960, the enrolments at the Technical Institute between 1954 and 1959 did not justify the expenditure of any considerable sum of money on the erection of engineering and construction workshops. He was '... *of the mind that students should be directed toward the Caernarvonshire Technical Institute, Bangor and the Denbighshire Technical College, Wrexham.*' Mindful, however, of the travelling distances involved, he suggested that the two workshops at Barberry Hill be retained for evening students only. For this reason, all provision for such courses was omitted from the building schedules designed for the new college.

The total area proposed was 56,750 sq. ft. which included:

- 25,050 sq. ft. for the main college
- 17,510 sq. ft. for the catering school
- 14,190 sq. ft. as circulation space for refectory, hall etc.

Even at this early stage, the schedules of proposed space were in excess of the allocated funding, which meant that re-adjustment became a major consideration.

On the 21st April 1961, the proposed schedule of accommodation for the new joint college, as prepared by the Ministry of Education, was again discussed by the Technical Institute's Policy & Reconstruction Committee. Of particular concern was the omission of any technical subjects other than agricultural machinery, the re-definition of the intended catchment area, and the fact that the owner of the intended site was concerned about the delay in concluding the negotiations. The response was clear: a workshop must be provided for first year technical students residing within the catchment area. This was later revised to two practical workshops to include first and second year technical and craft courses.

By December 1961, the budget proposals were being discussed, with a proportionate split of 42% for Caernarvonshire and 58% for Denbighshire, determined by the number of students from each county area.

Early in 1963, work began and seventeen months later in September 1964, Llandrillo Technical College opened its doors.

From the outset, the county architects of Denbighshire under the direction of Mr R.A. Macfarlane (county architect) and Mr E.R.P. Jones (project architect) were responsible for the design and build of the new college. With the advantage of a 'falling' site of some 50 feet, the architects were able to use the natural aesthetics to enable the building to overlook the golf course with the Little Orme and sea in the distance. The *North Wales Weekly News* reported on Thursday 24th June 1965: '*... of the many admirable features of Llandrillo Technical College not the least is the way it fits into the landscape so effectively.*'

The contract of approximately £320,000 was awarded to Gilbert-Ash Ltd, contractors from London. They built the college with INTERGRID, a process using precast concrete industrialised units which could be speedily erected by a small labour force. The external materials were kept to a minimum: essentially the white precast concrete aggregate panels, brickwork and local Dinorwic slate cladding. £50,000 was allocated for the purchase of land and legal charges and £35,000 for furniture and equipment, giving a total cost of £405,000.

The building programme was completed on time, although during the early excavation works there was concern that the whole project might be put on hold following the discovery of bones on the site. Further examination revealed the bones to be those of cattle, so work was allowed to resume!

The new College building comprised two main blocks as originally intended: a three storey block running east to west and a two storey block running north to south, adjoining the main road.

Most of the subjects transferring from Barberry Hill and Dinerth Road, including

Llandrillo Technical College, photographed in 1965. Following a request from the Steering Committee, the County Architect arranged for the name of the College in Welsh to be fixed alongside the English name. This was done in time for the official opening.

hairdressing, moved into the three storey 'main block', as it became known. The architects visited several other colleges to ensure the rooms for the only hairdressing department in North Wales were designed for purpose; the resulting state-of-the-art facilities were a major factor in the rising enrolment patterns of the future.

The two storey block housed the staff and students' dining room, kitchen and stores on the ground floor. The Department of Hotel Keeping & Catering on the first floor was claimed to be the first purpose-built teaching department in Wales and capable of offering full-time training to 150 students. Again, the architects visited other colleges in England, namely the Manchester School of Food and the South Devon College in Torquay, to ensure the building met the demands of the trade. An unusual feature for a college catering department at the time was the licensed public restaurant with a separate entrance. The Project Architect remembers a generous donation of £1,000 to incorporate the bar, which was said to be the first of its kind in any educational training establishment. This is supported by a record in the minutes of the College Steering Committee dated 30th November 1964, saying that the bar and fittings had been supplied free of charge by the National Trade Development Association.

The Catering Department was hailed as one of the most imaginative educational experiments in Wales. Experts came from far and wide to look at the superbly equipped kitchens and the training programmes that would generate the world-class chefs of the future. In the March 1967 edition of *Hotel & Restaurant Manager*, the College came under close scrutiny as the author enjoyed lunch in the Restaurant: '*A large airy room which provides a mural like view of the Little Orme and a glimpse of the sea.*' He complimented the students for their charm and keenness to serve and spoke keenly about the students' training making an immediate contribution to an establishment's popularity and profits!

Attached to the three storey block was the assembly hall/gymnasium with a

The main entrance to the new College.

fully equipped stage for drama work, plus student changing rooms for drama, gymnastics and outdoor recreation. Also within the new buildings was an inner courtyard. This housed the electricity substation, oil storage and boiler house and acted as a service area for deliveries, refuse etc., all out of sight of the public. One final addition was the Resident Steward's bungalow adjoining the car park.

When the College opened, there were no completed workshops. Whilst the initial building schedules did not include any, the plans had been revised to include a new workshop block, but this proved to be problematic. A communication from the Department of Education & Science in October 1964 instructed the college to end the current workshop block extension with the existing contractor and seek new tenders, the prices of which were to be no more than £17,516 gross.

Indeed, even at the time of the official opening in June 1965, the site remained clear: some early foundations and two metre high walls were demolished prior to the visit of Prince Philip and the appointment of the new contractor. Staff recall the frustrations and difficulties in agreeing the workshop specifications, and the Project Architect remembers the conflict he faced between the initial omission of the workshops, reducing budgets and workshop requirements, which were all at odds with each other. It is said that some nine drawings had been submitted before agreement was reached on the final specification, which inevitably added to the delays in construction. The delays created serious problems for the College, as teaching for the majority of the engineering and construction students had to continue at Barberry Hill. Finally, in the summer of 1966, staff were told to organise the transfer of their own equipment and furniture to the new workshops at the main site. For the Motor Vehicle Section, it proved to be an abortive effort: their equipment simply did not fit! They had to return, complete with their load, back to Barberry Hill. Later in the year, some of the Motor Vehicle staff and students moved again, to a hastily erected and extremely cold area situated to the rear of the workshops – christened the 'Ponderosa'. It was not until September 1968, with the provision of another new workshop that the remaining Motor Vehicle students finally relocated to the College site in Rhos.

It is not known exactly when the college finished using Barberry Hill but it is known that in January 1972, the staff and 225 children of Ysgol Bod Alaw left Rivieres Avenue and moved to Barberry Hill, following once again in the footsteps of Further Education in Colwyn Bay.

College Organisation

The internal organisation of the College became fully operational during the 1965/66 academic session. There were six departments:
• Commerce & Liberal Studies
• Construction & Engineering
• Domestic Subjects
• Hairdressing
• Hotel Keeping & Catering
• Science (including Nursing) & Maths

A presentation of art work.

The largest department was Commerce & Liberal Studies with 34% of total enrolments; the smallest was Science & Mathematics, which comprised only 4%.

Across the College, there were 46 full-time and 68 part-time lecturing staff, supported by 42 non-teaching staff.

Governance

Until March 1965, the College was governed by a Steering Committee pending the establishment of the Governing Body. In many respects, the Committee carried out the functions of the Governing Body whilst finalising the various articles and agreements that would govern the College. The formal document was entitled: 'Agreement relating to the establishment and management of the Joint Technical College at Llandrillo yn Rhos in the County of Denbigh'. It comprised three schedules:

1. The Instrument of Government which dealt with matters relating to the Governing Body;
2. The Articles of Government which dealt with issues of budgets, staffing and organisation and curriculum;
3. Financial arrangements which dealt with the methods of apportionments and re-charges enabling Denbighshire County Council to be the sponsoring Local Education Authority with responsibility for managing the accounts.

The Board had three standing committees:
- The Staffing Committee
- The Administrative Committee
- The Disciplinary Committee

The Welsh Office
A Welsh Office responsible to the Secretary of State for Wales was established in April 1965. It was not until 1978 however that it gained responsibility for further education.

Constitution of the Governing Body

The new Governing Body consisted of 30 members, of whom 28 were appointed by May 1965. Conspicuous by their absence were representatives from the Borough Council and worthy of note is the minute recorded at the General Purposes Committee of the Colwyn Bay Borough Council on Monday 12th October 1964: *'His Worship the Mayor reported that in his capacity as a Governor of the former Colwyn Bay Technical Institute he understood that there was to be no representation of this Council on the Board of Governors of the new Llandrillo Technical College ... and it was resolved that the Town Clerk be authorised to make strong representations to the Clerk of the Denbigh County Council that this omission should be rectified and a seat made available on the Board of Governors of the Llandrillo Technical College for one representative from this Council.'*

At the meeting of the Governing Body of Llandrillo Technical College on 28th May 1965 the Governors resolved that they could not accede to this request.

Constitution of Advisory Committees

In March 1965, the constitution of the Advisory Committees was approved. Each comprised either 10 or 11 members and included a member of the Governing Body:

1. Building Advisory Committee
2. Commerce & Liberal Studies Advisory Committee
3. Engineering Advisory Committee
4. Hairdressing Advisory Committee
5. Hotel & Catering Advisory Committee
6. Motor Vehicle Advisory Committee

Each Committee was required to nominate a representative for membership of the Governing Body which can be seen in the table opposite. The representative was not necessarily the Chair of the Advisory Committee as seen in the Hotel & Catering Advisory Committee where the Marquess of Anglesey had accepted the Chair of the Committee but did not sit on the Governing Body.

In February 1967, a meeting was convened to consider the Pre-Health Service Course.

Local Authority	Number	Member
Denbighshire LEA	8	
Caernarvonshire LEA	8	
Other North Wales LEAs Anglesey, Flintshire, Merionethshire and Montgomeryshire (1 each)	4	Mr Clarence Ellis, Mr Arthur Jones, Mr W.E. Jones, Mr J.A. Davies
Advisory Committees		
Building Committee	1	Mr F Tyldesley
Commerce & Liberal Studies	1	Mr P.G. Gadd
Engineering	1	Mr A.M. Livingstone, J.K. Smit & Sons Ltd
Hairdressing	1	Mr Leslie Roberts
Hotel & Catering	1	Mr E.L. Cox. Imperial Hotel
Motor Vehicle	1	Mr A Braid, Braid Bros.
Merseyside & North Wales Electricity Board (MANWEB)	1	Mr A.A.W. Hawley
Wales Gas Board	1	Mr J.F.Day
Two co-opted governors	2	

Whilst there is no recorded minute changing the status of this Committee, it is noted from the Board minutes in December 1968 that a seventh Advisory Committee had been introduced to the College governance – the Pre-Health Service Advisory Committee.

Composition of the new Governing Body.

No record has been found explaining why two of the six departments – Domestic Subjects and Science & Mathematics – did not have Advisory Committees whilst Engineering & Construction had three!

Financial agreement

In accordance with Schedule 3 of the Agreement made between the two County Councils, it was agreed that annual expenditure should be apportioned between them in accordance with the population of the catchment area, for which the latest population census report of the Registrar General would be used. The catchment areas were defined as follows:

Denbighshire:
The Boroughs of Colwyn Bay & Denbigh
The Urban Districts of Abergele & Llanrwst
The Rural Districts of Aled & Hiraethog

Caernarvonshire:
The Borough of Conway
The Urban Districts of Betws y Coed,
 Llandudno & Penmaenmawr
The Rural District of Nant Conwy

The method of apportionment was adopted for a period of three years, with each review to take effect from the following financial year commencing 1st April. Denbighshire was the sponsoring authority, administering all financial matters; Caernarvonshire was required to pay a quarterly advance of funds based on the annual estimates and to recompense Denbighshire for its services.

The net expenditure for 1964/65 was £101,699 with 42% of the cost falling to Caernarvonshire and 58% of the costs falling to Denbighshire. In 1965/66, net expenditure had risen to £180,634.

In September 1970, the basis of apportionment of charges was amended, partly on the basis of the total rateable values of the catchment areas and partly on the basis of student hours.

The Official Opening by HRH Prince Philip

The official opening of the College in 1965 marked not only a new era in Further Education but the diamond jubilee of Further Education within the Colwyn Bay area.

Preparations for the Prince's visit had been extensive and clearly occupied the Principal, Mr W.J. Griffiths, and his Chair of the Board of Governors, Mr D.B. Jones, for many months, as evidenced by the Principal's 'Official Opening' file. Records indicate that a small sub-committee planned all the arrangements, with the Director of Education for Denbighshire responsible for official invitations. A limit of 400 guests in the Assembly Hall was clearly a major challenge. With two local authorities involved, numbers continually exceeded the available seating space resulting in many communications being necessary to control final numbers.

At 3.50 p.m. on Wednesday, 23rd June 1965, two helicopters of the Queen's Flight arrived slightly later than planned, carrying HRH Prince Philip, the Lord Lieutenant Col J.C. Wynne Finch and the Director of Education for Denbighshire, Mr T.G. Davies MA, BSc. They had flown in from Llysfasi Farm Institute, Ruthin, where the Prince had made an hour-long stop as part of a two day tour of Denbighshire. In the words of the June 1965 edition of *Technical Outlook*, the official journal of the Caernarvonshire and Llandrillo Technical Colleges, *'Crowds had been gathering outside the main gates of the College for about two hours; troops of Scouts, Guides and Sea Rangers and a large proportion of the Local*

Making his way across the College playing fields, HRH Prince Philip arrives for the official opening by helicopter.

HRH Prince Phillip is welcomed to the College by the reception party. He is shown here shaking hands with Mr D.B. Jones, Chair of the Governing Body.

Constabulary were lined up on duty, and four hundred or so dignitaries, VIPs and townspeople were in the main hall and the foyer, when that exciting moment, for which preparations had been going on for the past weeks, arrived.

A cheer went up as the red helicopter piloted by the Duke himself landed behind the College. Students' faces appeared at all the windows as the Duke came round to the front entrance where he was introduced to Mr Griffiths, Principal, looking very scholastic in his robes and mortar board, and other officials.'

The two and a half hour event went as planned despite a strong wind which threatened the spectacle of the arriving helicopters. Prince Philip commented in his address: '... *I arrived as you may have noticed in one of the latest technical devices, but it is powerless to advance at any great rate against a strong wind ...'*

A beneficiary of the wind however was the newly erected flagstaff at the college entrance.

A reception party of eight dignitaries greeted the Prince as he arrived on the sports pitch, all of whom were officially presented by the Lord Lieutenant. The dignitaries included the Mayor of Colwyn Bay, Mrs E.B. Jones who was introduced alongside her husband, Mr D.B. Jones, Chairman of the Governing Body.

The day was primarily one of ceremony and as the reception party entered the foyer, the plaque was unveiled to commemorate the visit to an audience of some 50 guests and 20 students.

LLANDRILLO TECHNICAL COLLEGE
OPENED BY
H.R.H. THE PRINCE PHILIP,
DUKE OF EDINBURGH,
K.G., K.T.

23 JUNE, 1965.

The guests then proceeded into the main hall, where fifteen of the stage party mounted the platform and led proceedings to a packed audience of over 400 guests, which included official reporters and the BBC.

The Chairman of the Governing Body opened proceedings and gave an address of welcome. This was followed by a Service of Dedication which included a passage from the scriptures read by the Reverend Gwilym I. Davies, BA, BD, Vice President of the Llandudno Free Church Council, and prayers by the Reverend E.D. Evans, BA, Vicar of Llandrillo-yn-rhos, and the Reverend Father Lawrence Whittle, OMI, Colwyn Bay. The Chairman then spoke, stating, '... *I am confident that the expenditure involved in building and equipping this new college at a cost of something like £350,000 can be seen to be fully justified ...*' before inviting Prince Philip to address the guests and declare the College officially open. Sometime during these proceedings, the College confirmed its intention to retain the already established motto of the Technical Institute – 'O Grefft i Gryfder'.

In his address, His Royal Highness spoke passionately about technical education and from the transcripts held he is noted as saying: '... *it takes considerable technical qualifications just to keep the equipment of this modern world functioning and reliable.*'

Prior to the close of the ceremony, two presentations were made to Prince Philip, both very different in content. Mr Victor C. Wilde, JP, a major benefactor of the College, presented a deed stating that he would convey to Denbighshire Education Committee an area of approximately 12 acres of adjoining land to be solely used for recreational purposes. Alderman R.E. Rowlands, JP, Chairman of Denbighshire County Council, presented a silver horse's head drinking cup which he hoped the Prince would remember from his visit to Denbighshire.

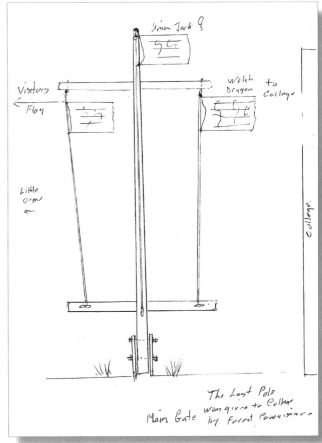

A sketch of the College flag pole by Mr H.W. Edmondson, Resident Caretaker (January 1968 – July 1987).

HRH Prince Philip tours the handicraft area (right) and meets the 'hat makers'.

Following the vote of thanks by Alderman Goronwy Owen, JP, Chairman of Denbighshire Education Committee, and Alderman Hugheston Roberts, Chairman of the Caernarvonshire Education Committee, the proceedings ended with the singing of the two national anthems, 'Hen Wlad fy Nhadau' and 'God save the Queen'.

Prince Philip was then taken on a tour of the College along a well-planned route that covered most areas of college activity. To ensure the tour was of interest not only to the royal guest but the many other guests in attendance, each area had made special preparations, which included wig making in the hairdressing department, hat making in the handicraft area, making beds in the home management area, dissecting rats in the science department and the caterers carrying out cookery presentations concluding with afternoon tea in the restaurant.

Such was the importance of the day that companies from far and wide loaned equipment to the College: two Austin vehicles, two models of Industrial Meters plus the school meals equipment necessary to ensure sufficient crockery for entertaining the guests.

HRH Prince Philip addresses guests of Llandrillo Technical College in the main hall.

To mark the occasion, staff and students of the catering department had made a magnificent cake iced with Prince Philip's official crests and the words 'Many Happy Returns' to mark the occasion of the Prince's birthday on 10th June.

Detailed lists of students, classrooms and pre-prepared students' activities were planned well in advance of the day and all students were to be occupied in their teaching area. Strict instructions were issued to each lecturer to avoid unplanned activity, and only when the Prince was aboard the helicopter ready for departure were students to be allowed onto the playing fields to give him a *'hearty send off'*.

Most students were not required in college until 2.00 p.m. but for those who were required to attend, the lunch hour was extended. Needless to say, such excitement in the college could not be contained and staff were alerted to the arrival/return of many inebriated students who had enjoyed the longer than normal lunch hour in the nearby public house. The event was unaffected; these students were conveniently removed and left to recover in the toilets or the catering swill room!

The final part of the Prince's busy schedule that day was his flight to the school field in Pentrefoelas, following which he was escorted by car to the home of Colonel Finch and his wife.

Concluding his two day tour of Denbighshire the next day, Prince Philip attended the Duke of Edinburgh Awards' Rally in Eirias Park followed by a visit to the Civic Centre before his departure. Over 600 young people gathered in Eirias Park displaying the skills and activities offered by the Scheme. Also present was Lord John Hunt, First Director of the Duke of Edinburgh Award Scheme, who led the first team to climb Mount Everest, paving the way for Edmund Hillary to reach the summit.

The minutes of the General Purposes Committee of the Borough of Colwyn Bay on 12th April 1965 stated: *'It was desired to know whether the Council would provide a Buffet Lunch for the Duke of Edinburgh*

A birthday cake for HRH Prince Philip.

A hearty send-off from the crowd as HRH Prince Philip makes his way to the helicopters for the next stage of his journey.

HRH Prince Philip meets the hairdressers.

and his party together with probably 75 - 100 leaders of the Award Scheme.' The proposal was accepted and the Entertainments Manager approached the College for their services; the catering students and staff duly obliged.

5. The Late Sixties – Responding to Student Needs

Student Growth during the Late Sixties

The enrolment statistics laid out in the Annual Reports show a steady growth in student numbers during the late sixties:

Mode of attendance	Barberry Hill/ Hotel School	LTC	LTC	LTC
	'63/'64	'64/'65	'68/'69	'69/'70
Full-time	268	354	496	522
Part-time	507	528	945	636
Evening	954	970	2,226	1,494
TOTAL	1,729	1,852	3,667	2,652

By 1968/69, College enrolments had risen to 3,667, although various changes in reporting add a degree of caution to the interpretation of the statistics: a changing method of recording for day-time recreational classes plus a departmental reorganisation in readiness for the 1969/70 academic session. Whilst full-time numbers had almost doubled to over 500 students by 1969/70, the drop to 2,652 total enrolments in that year was, it is claimed, the consequence of an increase in non-vocational tuition fees and a greatly reduced evening programme.

All six departments of the College were developing strongly with demand and competition for resources continuing to grow. Each year, student activity was measured and presented as a 'unit total', in line with the calculations laid down in the

Burnham Education Report. In 1969, the 'unit total' increased and the academic work of the College was reorganised into four departments, each categorised as Grade 2 for the determination of staffing purposes:

- Commerce & Liberal Studies
- Engineering, Construction & Science
- Fashion & Health
- Hotel Keeping & Catering

Commerce & Liberal Studies

This was the largest of all the Departments with approximately 600 enrolments. It covered all aspects of commerce as well as the provision of languages and liberal studies to all full-time students. Full-time enrolment remained fairly constant in the early years whilst evening provision grew rapidly. The area had a Head of Department, 10 full-time lecturing staff supported by 22 part-time lecturing staff rising to 13 full-time lecturing staff by 1970.

Each year, an annual review of local industries provided the evidence for curriculum change. The newly emerging Training Boards demanded greater management training and improved training for office clerks. As technology impacted upon the modern office, the design of courses was continually reviewed to embrace the introduction of new audio techniques and the mechanisation of equipment in general.

The Commerce & Liberal Studies Department provided a much-needed internal service to other departments of the College including management training, languages and business. In 1967/8, liberal studies was extended to all full-time students who were offered three different, termly sessions of 1.5 hours' additional teaching in subjects such as introductory science, hair care, current affairs, art, drama, dressmaking, home management, Italian and more.

The Department worked closely with schools and industry alike but despite this the full-time diploma courses struggled each year to recruit healthy numbers, with a further constraint introduced in

Students benefit from the new typewriting rooms.

Industrial Training Board needed management training, four courses were designed, each of which fully recruited.

As numbers continued to grow, the Department benefited from the building programme in 1969, with an additional typewriting room, an office practice room, a language laboratory and 3 new classrooms. The language laboratory comprising 20 language booths and a master console paved the way for the introduction of ten week intensive courses in French and Business to help local businesses prepare for Britain's entry to the EEC in 1973.

Domestic Subjects

1970/71 as the new Coleg Meirionnydd, Dolgellau opened its doors. Part-time day-release courses also struggled but despite such uncertainty, the Department was responsive and capable of creating new courses as demand required. When the civil servants dwindled to nil they were quickly replaced with police cadets from the new police headquarters in Gwynedd, who were offered a bespoke training programme over two days. Similarly when the Engineering

When Llandrillo Technical College opened, this was the second largest department with approximately 550 enrolments, predominantly in non-vocational classes, a consequence of the number of enrolments in needlework-related subjects transferring from the Technical Institute in 1964. The number of staff rose quickly from 3 full-time and 15 part-time lecturing staff to 24 staff in total by 1966/67. For management purposes, the area was broadly split into three: Fashion, Food & the Family and Embroidery.

Accommodation was restricted to a kitchen, a home management room and three craft rooms. The lack of available accommodation was mentioned

Handicraft items on display at the College Open Day

frequently in the annual reports of the Department, which was frustrated by the use of the home management room for general lectures by other areas of the College. The issues relating to space were made even worse by the lack of a covered area between the kitchen and home management area – a problem when the weather was inclement.

Growth was difficult given the space restrictions although the area did see expansions in dressmaking and cookery

plus the development of a partnership arrangement between the Llysfasi Farm Institute and the Rural Domestic Economy class. Full-time enrolments, initially relating to a two-year domestic science course, increased from 21 to over 45 following the introduction of a new full-time dressmaking course.

Despite the accommodation issues, the Domestic Subjects Department produced a range of commendable outcomes for the students, who secured positions throughout

England and Wales ranging from dressmakers, cooks and assistant cooks to housekeepers and house parents. Indeed, the annual Open Day was an occasion to show off, with a fashion parade and a splendid display of cookery, handicrafts, millinery and embroidery.

In 1969/70, in conjunction with the recommendations of the Burnham Committee Technical report, the Governors merged the Department of Domestic Subjects within the newly formed Department of Fashion & Health which was to become responsible for hairdressing, pre-health, domestic subjects,

Mr Quinton Hazell delivers the opening speech at the College Open Day and Prize Distribution, focusing on the need to create the technical skills to meet the future.

art and physical education making it the largest of the four departments at the turn of the decade. An item of note which remains without explanation is the lack of an Advisory Committee afforded to this area in these early years.

Engineering & Construction

Similar in size to the Domestic Subjects Department, the component divisions of the Engineering & Construction Department were Engineering, Construction and Motor Vehicle. Each section was treated separately for reporting purposes, with its own Advisory Committee that played an active role in determining the needs of the local industry. There was no Head of Department because overall numbers were considered too small for such an appointment.

This Department faced immediate challenges as soon as the College opened because it began its existence without dedicated workshop areas. By 1966, new workshops were ready for use but for some students, insufficient space meant a continuation of their studies at Barberry Hill until 1968 when new additional space became available. Despite the issues arising from the accommodation shortfall, the area continued to grow in strength, a consequence mainly of the Industrial Training Act 1966 and the creation of the Industrial Training Boards. By 1967/68, the Department as a whole was working with five different Training Boards.

During the College reorganisation in 1969/70, Engineering & Construction grew to include Science, and became the second largest department in the College with some 750 enrolments.

The Engineering Section—The early years saw continued use of the Barberry Hill site until the new workshop areas were ready in 1966. The retention of the gas courses after months of averting their transfer to the Flintshire Technical College and the introduction of the integrated courses combining further education and apprenticeship training established a platform for future development.

Within the Engineering Section there were 200 students: 30 were full-time pre-apprentices, a number that swelled to 50 with the introduction of the Engineering Industrial Training Board (EITB) course in 1968/69, 60 were gas fitters from the Wales Gas Board on block-release programmes and the remaining 100 were part-time day/evening students.

The gas courses attracted students from across Wales and each year the Section had to draw on local hotels to provide lodgings for 60-70 students. The newly constructed gas fitting workshop at Rhos had been a major beneficiary of the bespoke training programmes and this, together with the organisation and management of this discrete number of students, had been a major factor in averting the transfer of provision to Flintshire.

Celebrating the retention of the gas courses however was short-lived. By 1967/68, changes to the structure of the gas courses by the Gas Industry Training Board led to a reduction in numbers, as the traditional four year training programmes were reduced to a three year programme. By 1969/70, with the College reorganisation, the Section lost the provision altogether as the courses transferred to Construction. Sadly, things did not improve for the Construction Section, which saw a continued fall in student numbers with the introduction of the Selective Employment Tax (SET) and the centralisation of gas training in Wales to Cardiff in 1971.

Students at work in the gas fitting workshop.

The newly created Engineering Industrial Training Board however was influential,

immediately creating its own courses for the engineering students of the future. Bespoke courses were also designed to meet the needs of the Fire Service in basic electricity and Quinton Hazell, a local company. Creativity was a key component in the development of these courses, not least the course on colour television, which called for improvision because the College did not have a colour television!

Newly built open-plan workshops, in use from 1966, came with a major problem – noise! All three disciplines for both practical and theory classes were initially located in one workshop. There was constant dialogue between management and the authorities on the modifications and rationalisation needed to enable theory classes to take place without interruptions from machine noise generated in the practical courses. Construction and Motor Vehicle expressed similar concerns. For over five years, this issue remained central to the annual budgetary discussions within the Department, resulting in further new workshops or extensions and alterations up to and including the early '70s.

In 1967/68, the Department piloted the introduction of 'Programmed Learning' – recorded material for use in the classroom. During 1969/70, two engineering programmes were completed as aides in the classroom – 'Tinning the Bit' and 'Soldering', both programmes shown to the students using a projector and tape recorder.

The Construction Section—The early years of Construction comprised the carpenters, joiners and plumbers. Painting & Decorating, although originally intended to move from Bethlehem Church Hall, Lawson Road, to Barberry Hill failed to recruit sufficient numbers and the provision ceased. At a meeting of the Llandrillo Technical College Steering Committee on 9th October 1964, a decision was made to terminate the lease of Bethlehem Church Hall as the low enrolments could no longer warrant its continuation. The painters and decorators finished their programmes in Lawson Road that year and waited a further two years before the courses were re-introduced at the annexe in Barberry Hill in September 1966 which coincided with

the engineering students leaving for the College site and a new workshop.

By 1966/67, there were 11 full-time pre-apprentices and 170 students across day/evening programmes, the numbers boosted by the 16 returning painters and decorators. Four year programmes were available for the plumbers and a fifth year had been introduced for the carpentry and joinery students enabling them to qualify at the advanced craft certificate level. 'Programmed Learning' had been introduced and short bespoke courses were being run for the then Conway Valley Water Board, the Development Association for Lead together with a short course on 'metrication' for the industry as a whole.

Carpentry and joinery students benefit from the new equipment.

In 1968, following the erection of a second workshop, part of the Construction Section transferred to a new open area, fondly christened the 'Giraffe House' which was essentially a roof supported by four pillars! This rationalisation of the remaining space finally allowed the remaining twelve Motor Vehicle (RTITB) students to transfer from Barberry Hill to the main site.

Whilst enrolments remained constant, there was concern that employers were not releasing apprentices to attend college and there was increasing pressure to improve initial course enrolments. In 1964, the National Advisory Council on Education for Industry & Commerce had established a committee on the more effective use of technical college resources. Its first report, known as the Pilkington Report after the committee's first chairman, had decreed that courses should not run without a minimum class size of 15. In the more rural College catchment areas this often meant courses were not allowed to run, forcing students to travel longer distances to the college in Flintshire. One casualty of such a ruling was the radio and television course which only had 7 students.

The Construction Industrial Training Board (CITB) was slower than the EITB to change from day-release programmes to block-release and off-the-job training. To the detriment of the Section, the annual intake of apprentices fell with painting and decorating remaining a concern. The Advisory Committee worked pro-actively with the industry and the CITB to improve recruitment and in 1969/70, supported the submission of plans to rationalise the construction workshops to facilitate improved planning and delivery of courses.

The changing nature of the building trades towards the end of the sixties led to some major challenges for the Construction Section as they entered the seventies. These included the loss of trainees resulting from the imposition of the selective employment tax on construction companies and the decision by the Wales Gas Board to set up their own training base in Cardiff.

The Motor Vehicle Section—despite being the smallest of the three sections in terms of enrolments, faced exactly the same challenges in terms of accommodation as the other two. Whilst support for the agricultural mechanics course, the only such course in North Wales, had been secured at the outset, the Section faced a continuing challenge to secure workshop space at the College in Rhos. In 1965/66, there were no full-time enrolments. All courses were part-time and included 74 motor vehicle mechanics training over three years, 21 agricultural mechanics training over two years and 40 owner drivers training in the evening.

The area was keen to develop pre-apprenticeship courses but initially, poor accommodation and insufficient sustainable numbers meant no full-time students started in this era.

The first of the motor vehicle students arrived at College from Barberry Hill in 1966, followed by the remaining twelve Road Transport Industrial Training Board (RTITB) students in 1968 in space created by the opening of the second new workshop. New buildings were also added to the rear of the existing workshop comprising a covered area, a lock-up garage

Motor Vehicle students with a Triumph Herald.

and a petroleum store – an area to become affectionately known for many years as the 'Ponderosa'. For the early students who transferred, their most vivid memories of the Ponderosa area were the 'makeshift' workshop, created from three walls and a roof, with no heat during the winter months as they arrived at the main site.

The area was also of great importance as a space for developing new courses in readiness for the annual discussions on course provision. What better way to provide evidence of your future requirements? In 1968/69, the donation of an ex-removal van from Brookes of Rhyl was a great step forward as it resolved the problem of a classroom for many years.

In terms of enrolments, there was little overall change in the early years of the College despite the best efforts of the three full-time lecturers, who were extremely pro-active in visiting the local garages and shows every year to recruit new students.

The integrated courses were introduced in 1969/70 as was welding, which transferred from Engineering. It was a time when new courses developed but it was also a time when some simply ceased to enrol. The agricultural courses ceased, as did the approval for the 168 Part III Compression Ignition Course which was withdrawn by the DES in 1970. Its subsequent transfer to Bangor Technical College disappointingly never succeeded in recruiting, so the area was left without such provision for many years. Whilst active in many ways, the RTITB was slow in announcing grants to the industry and

the removal of the small garages from the grants levy system meant student numbers remained at similar levels each year.

By 1970, the area had swelled to 5 full-time staff, 3 part-time staff and 1 technician.

The Hairdressing Department

Despite being referred to as the Hairdressing Department for most of the sixties, the Department comprised not only hairdressing but also art and physical education courses. For the most part, the three areas operated quite independently although the full-time hairdressing students were required to participate in aspects of art and physical education as part of their liberal studies programmes.

There were approximately 130 hairdressing students and over 200 part-time/evening students studying art and physical education. The hairdressing facilities included two fully-equipped salons, which attracted students from all over North Wales. Enrolments during the early years remained fairly constant although it is noticeable that part-time courses did fluctuate year on year. The Department also had a Hairdressing Advisory Committee which restricted itself to hairdressing matters.

The Hairdressing Section—attracted considerable interest from local and national organisations, with several larger organisations using the College as a base for their national events. During 1966/67, the Hairdressing Teachers Inter College Competition Finals were held at the Grand Hotel in Llandudno, using the College as their preparatory base. In 1969/70, Miss Kay Welstead, World Champion Stylist, provided a demonstration of her skills at the College on behalf of Wella UK.

The salons appear to have been well maintained but like other areas of the College, space was limited for the theoretical parts of the education programmes. The Annual Reports

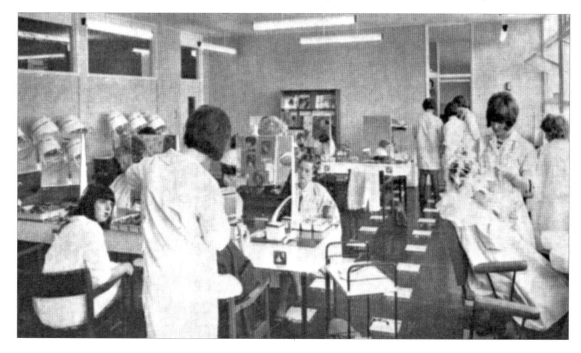

Students at work in the hairdressing salon.

constantly highlight the problems of the theory classes being held in the refectory or the students' common room. The portfolio of courses was updated regularly and included the introduction of men's hairdressing and aspects of beauty therapy for the existing students. Theatrical makeup and charm and poise courses were also successfully added to the evening portfolio. A new reception desk was introduced in the salons in 1969/70, built by the students of the Construction Section.

No new full-time courses were introduced because of the space restrictions but progress was being made towards the future introduction of beauty therapy courses. Work experience was a challenge to the staff of the hairdressing department as many of their students were not local to the College. This meant inspection visits were seldom carried out in advance of the placement and correspondence tended to be by letter. These procedures were recognised as being unsatisfactory, particularly as work experience was a necessary requirement for the students as part of their curriculum.

Full-time students enjoying their liberal studies programmes in the art rooms.

The Art Section—consisted primarily of two elements: the servicing of full-time students, primarily hairdressing students plus afternoon and evening provision in dedicated art space. The area was constantly under pressure from the timetabling demands of other areas within the College. Succumbing to such pressure, two classes actually moved out to Barberry Hill in 1967/68 to ensure space was guaranteed. With the introduction of the liberal studies entitlement for full-time students, art classes increased – as did the requests for additional money to provide adequate materials.

The Physical Education Section— struggled with accommodation from the beginning. With only the main hall and two pitches available, the Section spent their early years attempting to increase and improve upon the facilities available to enhance physical education for all students of the College in general. Facilities included a football pitch and a hockey pitch but both suffered from constant flooding during the winter months making them unusable for large parts of the academic

year. Athletics was also generally frustrated by long grass and inadequate markings making practice very difficult. The main hall, which was expected to accommodate all aspects of physical education, was marked out for badminton purposes and simply stored various items of gymnastic and other equipment. Initially, as both staff were female, it was felt that this was not beneficial to the full-time male students. That said, there was no shortage of male activities and many lecturers within the College played a key role in supporting the development of clubs and societies.

The main hall, host to a variety of activities.

The refectory.

timetabled together, for example the first year Commerce girls with the gas fitters from Construction.

Staff recall that the above-average replacement of light fittings in the hall was predominantly down to inappropriate sports use! They also remember that the introduction of the archery classes, whilst popular with the students, was much more worrying for the staff who were required to cross the area when using the toilets!

Hotel Keeping & Catering

With its state-of-the-art equipment and generous staffing levels, this purpose-built Department was intended from the outset to provide not only a programme of excellent training but also support and servicing for the local authorities and local businesses in hosting luncheons and ceremonies for visitors and guests to the area.

In comparison with other parts of the College, the Department was generously staffed with ten full-time lecturers, a number similar to that of the Commerce & Liberal

Despite inadequate resourcing, the area boasted football teams, rugby teams, cricket teams, five-a-side teams and more. Many entered local competitions and were fairly successful, despite a lack of practice facilities. The main hall was in constant use and was under pressure from competing demands: timetabling of the summer term examinations, Christmas functions, dances, local hirings and other events. Indeed, timetabling for physical education was often left to last, resulting in mixed and inappropriate groups of students being

Studies Department, which was twice its size. This reflected the predominance of practical classes across several food-related disciplines and the importance attached to the culinary provision. In the first two years, enrolments were evenly balanced, with 100+ full-time students matched by an equal number of part-time students. Over the next few years this was to change as full-time student numbers outstripped part-time numbers giving a total enrolment of over 300 students by 1969/70.

One of its first challenges was to appoint a new Head of Department. The Advisory Committee played a key role in the selection process but despite two attempts to recruit, no appointment was made. At a specially convened meeting in December 1965, it was agreed that in combining the work of the refectory within the Department, this Head of Department could justifiably be upgraded to a Level Two post. A successful appointment was announced soon afterwards.

The Advisory Committee was extremely pro-active and was instrumental in working

with the Department to approve the early 'Student Services Schemes' which involved details of practical experience and the requirement for students to purchase their own set of knives. The schemes provided the guidelines for practical experience to be undertaken within the industry in the evening. This requirement was in addition to the special functions hosted in the Training restaurant. By

The Orme View restaurant as it was in the eighties, fundamentally the same as when it opened.

Catering students at work.

The very first of the Epicurean dinners boasting an exquisite menu.

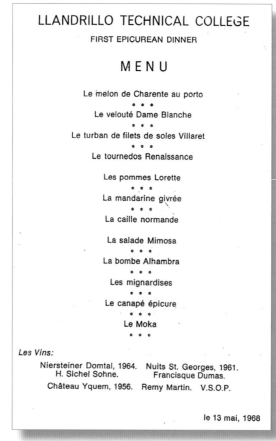

LLANDRILLO TECHNICAL COLLEGE

FIRST EPICUREAN DINNER

MENU

Le melon de Charente au porto
* * *
Le velouté Dame Blanche
* * *
Le turban de filets de soles Villaret
* * *
Le tournedos Renaissance

Les pommes Lorette
* * *
La mandarine givrée
* * *
La caille normande

La salade Mimosa
* * *
La bombe Alhambra
* * *
Les mignardises
* * *
Le canapé épicure
* * *
Le Moka
* * *

Les Vins:

Niersteiner Domtal, 1964.   Nuits St. Georges, 1961.
    H. Sichel Sohne.   Francisque Dumas.
Château Yquem, 1956. Remy Martin. V.S.O.P.

le 13 mai, 1968

In 1968, the Epicurean, perhaps the most innovative and challenging event of the College year was launched. Its success was immediate and it quickly became a major event each year for the Governing Body and their guests.

Initially, the main course structures included the three year Craft courses and National Diploma and the two year HCI Intermediate which was later to be extended to a third year with full membership status of the Institute. By 1969/70, the National Diplomas were being phased out and replaced by the Ordinary National Diploma (OND) and the Higher National Diplomas (HND), and the HCI Intermediate was declared obsolete. The Department recruited its first intake on the OND in 1969/70 and its first intake onto the prestigious HND in 1970/71. At this time, Llandrillo Technical College was only one of twelve colleges approved to run the HND.

The Department was fortunate to have been provided with the most up-to-date facilities and equipment at the time of the

1966/67, around 12 special lunches were provided to a variety of organisations across North Wales, a number which was then maintained throughout the years. In 1967/68, the Department took part in the North Wales Catering Exhibition which lasted over one week.

College's opening, all of which was serviced annually and well maintained. Despite such facilities, the demand for accommodation grew quickly. Common to all areas of the College was the lack of teaching space and the requirement to incorporate the changes necessary to meet the changing needs of industry. This included the use of convection ovens, microwaves and the equipment needed to provide practical training in reception and office skills.

By 1970/71, full-time student numbers had doubled and the pressure on the existing resources was acute. The building programme of 1967/68 eased some of the pressures but the lack of capital funding for the remainder of the sixties meant that alternative strategies were needed. In 1970/71, the Department extended the teaching day simply to cope with the shortfall.

One area of concern raised by the Advisory Committee was the declaration that students did not remain in the industry for long after qualifying. In 1970, a major questionnaire was developed to confirm or disprove the situation. Of the 62% that responded, whilst some students did indeed leave, it also showed that initial employment was high with some 50% of students being employed locally in the first year and the remainder employed throughout England and Wales. The report also highlighted the fact that by the second year, students returned to Wales to work raising employment locally to 63%. The only area of disappointment was that 73% of those in employment received no further training – a factor that became an important consideration for the future.

Science, including Health and Mathematics

This was the smallest Department, with four full-time lecturers supported by nine part-time lecturers and one laboratory technician. The servicing of science and maths teaching across the College was its main function. Some 70% of the Department's total teaching hours serviced the Hotel Keeping & Catering, Hairdressing & Domestic Subjects departments, providing tuition in food, textiles, cosmetic and medical science.

The Secretary of State for Wales

On 24th May 1968, the College was visited by the Rt. Hon. George Thomas M.P. Secretary of State for Wales. After an inspection of the College, the Secretary of State enjoyed lunch with members of the Governing Body

The remainder of its work was divided between health and evening classes. In health, there were 30 students on a full-time two year pre-nursing course and 13 part-time nursing cadets. The evening enrolments comprised predominantly science O levels, photography classes and, latterly, seafaring-related courses requested by local sailing clubs which increased enrolments significantly from 122 in 1965/66 to over 200 in 1967/68.

With regard to the nursing programmes, the College worked closely with the matrons of the local hospitals and the Medical Officer of Health for Colwyn Bay County Borough Council. Placements were important for the second year pre-nursing students and the nursing cadets, and such close co-operation with the hospitals and the Borough provided important job opportunities for the students. The arrangement was reciprocal as the voluntary work undertaken by the students for one-day-a-week over 38 weeks often provided invaluable support services across the wards. The Department was keen to introduce work placements for all students, but the General Nursing Council was opposed to young people below the age of seventeen and a half years working on the wards.

The health students also performed an important function within the College by providing much needed support for the rota in the college's 'rest room'. Their duties included recording visits, nature of ailments and duration and assisting the Lecturer-in-Charge with the more minor ailments. In the spring term of 1970/71, the rest room had 340 student visitors – a number considered too high, resulting in much stricter controls against those presenting with more minor ailments.

The science laboratory.

By 1966/67, the Pre-Nursing programmes were replaced by the Pre-Health Service course which widened the breadth of the health-related aspects. The enrolments were encouraging and students were provided with a much wider range of hospital-related subjects and experience. In 1967/68, the College developed the Post Registration Ward Sisters' course in response to the Salmon Report. Despite careful planning and partnership, the first term's programme was postponed because the hospitals were unable to release staff to attend! By 1969/70, the situation was resolved and programmes successfully recruited each term. The introduction of Food Hygiene courses was also problematic in the early years as businesses were slow to develop training programmes for their employees.

The Department had three laboratories, all of which were fully utilised. With a shortage of teaching space across the College, the laboratories were often commandeered to accommodate theory-related classes of all disciplines. Requests were constantly made for a more dedicated room to assist with the nursing programmes and the issues were only resolved in the short term through the generosity of Llandudno General Hospital which loaned its specialist training room to the College once a month.

The Staff Association

The Staff Association was always an informal part of the college structure but, importantly for staff, it was a means of information, news and recreational activities. Each member paid an annual subscription and each operational area was represented on the Committee. The Committee organised a variety of activities, including the annual treasure hunt, activity weekends and the Christmas party, which operated continually until the nineties when it quietly slipped away.

The main hall played host to many a dance or concert. The Christmas party was a whole college affair. Organised primarily through the Hotel & Catering Department, operational areas were invited to provide the entertainment while the students were responsible for the stage management. Hairdressers danced, lecturers acted, choirs sang and Mr May, lecturer, performed his 'Tangerine' party piece, much to the delight of his audience and the Principal, Mr Griffiths.

The Students' Association

Whilst an association had existed to some extent for several years, 1968/69 saw the first real attempt to organise a more formalised Students' Association, with a designated common room, a social calendar built around sports fixtures, dances, a Christmas concert, a drama society and the first rag week in 1968 which raised over £600 for disabled children. A Student/Staff Liaison Committee was formed as part of the Association to act as a forum for discussion and greater understanding of student-related concerns.

A group of students and staff in 1965.

The End of the Sixties

Despite the additional investment, the sixties ended with a general frustration that accommodation was still inadequate to meet the demands of a growing student population. In 1969/70, the College's capital bid was extensive, but funding was already beginning to reduce and the Department of Education & Science did not release any major capital monies. In response, the College improvised and made do, seeking equipment from a variety of sources and developing new courses wherever possible. It was most definitely a time of innovation and eagerness to expand.

The Principal's Annual Report for the 1969/70 academic session was produced shortly after his decision to reorganise the academic work of the college from six departments to four departments as required by the Burnham Further Education Report 1969. Whilst extremely positive on the one hand, it outlined the variety of challenges faced by the steadily growing College:

- Inadequate space across all areas of the College requiring significant capital investment to meet the growing number of enrolments and maintain quality standards;
- The future impact of the school reorganisation in Denbighshire for 16-19 year olds where integrated sixth forms would impact upon enrolment trends requiring greater co-operation and school link programmes;
- The forthcoming raising of the school leaving age in 1972/73 with the likelihood of fewer two year programmes and more one year courses;
- The debilitating effect on local industry, a consequence of being denied grants for buildings and equipment by not being included in the Development Areas in North Wales (boundaries imposed by the Department of Employment and Productivity);
- Increasing numbers of students on integrated courses developed as part of the new Industrial Training Boards, placing pressure on daytime availability and changes to curriculum design;

- the introduction of the first HE programme in September 1970 – the HND in Hotel and Catering Administration;
- academic support services under pressure with the growing number of enrolments, e.g. library provision, student welfare needs, refectory, technical support in the classroom, physical education shortfall;
- demands for new staff in financial services to cope with the rising levels of cash from tuition fees and refectory sales;
- difficulties in recruitment, particularly of female staff for cleaning services and refectory areas. (Low rates of pay and expensive travel costs made cleaning of female areas particularly difficult.)

The early years of the new Llandrillo Technical College were therefore buoyant and challenging, with a significant growth in student enrolments set amidst considerable change resulting from a variety of different factors – external and political influences, relationships with employers and schools and the students themselves.

6. The Seventies – a Decade of Challenges

Despite the growth in student numbers outstripping the resources available, the early years of Llandrillo Technical College were clearly successful. Shortage of space was a constant issue for the Principal, Mr Griffiths, and a frustration for many staff who were attempting to respond to the changing demands in technical and vocational education.

The seventies provided further challenges, not least because of the imposition of continued changes in constitution, educational structures and curriculum development which did little to resolve the overcrowded classrooms. Gradually, things did improve and during the later years of the decade, the College was finally supported with the long awaited and enhanced building programme, despite the imposition of annual budgetary cuts.

In 1972, two significant constitutional changes occurred. Firstly, the Local Government Act reformed local government in England and Wales, reducing the 13 counties of Wales to 8 new county councils supported by 36 district councils. This change, with some marginal boundary changes, essentially replaced the Denbighshire and Caernarvonshire authorities with Clwyd County Council and Gwynedd County Council. Constitutionally therefore, from 1st April 1974, the College was managed by two different authorities.

Also in 1972, new instruments and articles of government for the College were introduced, allowing staff and student representation on the College Governing Body for the first time. The changes also included the introduction of an Academic Board as part of the organisational structure of the college, which enabled staff to contribute effectively to academic developments. Further changes followed in 1974, when the new County Councils began to function.

Alongside these constitutional changes, staff terms and conditions were also reviewed. New conditions of service were developed for teachers with the Association of Teachers in Technical Institutions (ATTI) and the Council of Local Authorities, and a job evaluation survey was carried out on the administration of the college. The survey resulted in an increase in staff numbers, a positive but costly outcome at a time when the budget was being reduced.

Curriculum developments were moving swiftly to take into account the demands of a changing economy and rising unemployment allied to the more pressing needs of the College's local communities. The well-established narrow-based courses faced rejection in favour of learning by way of integrated study and modular delivery. There was a demand for more block-release courses, short intensive courses and one year courses to replace the traditional two year courses and sandwich courses. The changes were welcomed by the College and described as *'exciting and stimulating'* by the Principal.

On 31st August 1976, following 22 years of energising service to the Technical Institute and Llandrillo Technical College, the Principal, Mr Griffiths, retired and a new era began. His successor was the recently appointed Vice Principal, Mr

William Geoffrey Sparrow. Mr Sparrow, like his predecessor, was also a graduate of the University College, Aberystwyth, where he gained honours degrees in Law and Geography. Prior to his appointment

as Vice Principal, he was Head of the Business Studies Department at Chester College of Further Education and before that he held posts at Huddersfield Teacher Training College and St Albans and Crawley Further Education Colleges.

Promotion for Mr W.G. Sparrow as he becomes the new Principal of Llandrillo Technical College.

Mr J.A.K. Brown,
Vice Principal.

The position of Vice Principal was filled by Mr J.A.K. Brown, an Honours graduate in Science from Strathclyde University. Mr Brown was the former Head of Department of Mechanical & Civil Engineering at Stow College, Glasgow.

Both appointments were made in time for the start of the 1976/77 academic session.

Educational Changes

In addition to the changes in constitution and senior staff positions, there were several key educational developments and initiatives in the seventies which also had a major impact on the development of the College. These included:

- The raising of the school leaving age in September 1972 which meant that no students would be eligible to attend a technical college until they reached the age of 16 from September 1973.
- New school link courses at College to enable pupils to experience the requirements of industry and commerce and assist them in their future choice of career. During 1972/73, five secondary schools participated in a pilot link programme referred to as ROSLA (Raising of the School Leaving Age).
- A reduction in the teaching year from 39 weeks to 38 weeks which impacted on the availability of lecturing staff.
- The reorganisation by the new Clwyd Authority of the 'old Denbighshire Further and Higher Education establishments' in the east. This created an Institute of Higher Education (the then North Wales Institute) comprising the old Denbighshire Technical College, the old Flintshire Technical College and the Cartrefle College of Education.
- The reorganisation of further education in Gwynedd which had a major impact upon local catchment areas and forced many students from Gwynedd away from Llandrillo Technical College.
- The emergence of the Technician Education Council (TEC) and the Business Education Council (BEC). They now controlled curricular development and became the award-giving bodies for technician level courses. Ordinary National Certificates/Diplomas were

replaced with BEC General and National Diplomas.

- A Training Award Scheme introduced by the Department of Employment and the Industrial Training Boards, sponsoring places for the young unemployed in Engineering and Hotel Keeping & Catering.
- A Training Opportunities Scheme introduced for unemployed adults supported entirely by the Department of Employment including office studies and general catering courses.
- A Government Vocational Training Scheme introduced to expand the provision of training courses and to widen the range of training for industrial occupations.
- The creation of the Manpower Services Commission (MSC) in 1974 to look at issues of unemployment. The MSC effectively sidestepped local authority controls by using the Training Services Agency and the Employment Services Agency to provide services for which it became responsible. Essentially the MSC was set up to coordinate vocational training with responsibility to manage and expand the government's vocational training schemes, such as the Youth Opportunities Programme (YOPs) and the Training Opportunities Programme (TOPs), which offered retraining and skills development to adults intending to re-enter the workforce.

Budgetary Issues

The economy in the seventies was a period of rising inflation, increasing balance of payments deficits, unprecedented currency depreciation, rising unemployment and bitter industrial conflict. Tensions rose as local government services became subject to increased decision making by central government, with numerous measures to increase the efficiency of local authorities in administering their services. By 1976, cash limits imposed through the rate support grant meant that local authorities had to respond. Budgets were managed with a careful eye and each year there was evidence that the budgetary discussions were simply focused on which areas had to be cut to ensure compliance with government expectations.

The seventies also revealed the first hints of problems with the newly constituted Gwynedd County Council. In 1975, the Council capped their contribution to the College at £326,050 which resulted in a reduced budget of £68,000 impacting directly on course provision.

It was also a time when centrally funded organisations like the MSC, using monies previously in the control of the local authorities, demanded new approaches to serving the local labour market. Local authorities were required to be more responsive to the needs of their labour market and colleges had not only to bid for money to support their training programmes but they had to compete for resources against the private sector. Whilst never an intention to top slice such budgetary allocations, the MSC were clear that they would finance provision from whatever source, should the need not be met by the local authority. These new arrangements also came with a hidden cost – paperwork. The demand on College staff increased overnight and for years the curriculum areas pleaded for additional clerical support to assist in the completion of the many forms required to satisfy each of the different training strands.

Financial control became more complicated, not only because of the complexity of the funding streams but also by the need to ensure an adequate and appropriate resource allocation for a growing but slightly different type of student enrolment. The increases in full-time and day-release students were not only expensive in terms of staffing but increasingly, consumables budgets were placed under strain. Laundry bills grew, as did the materials needed for the workshops and the classrooms.

Enrolments had grown rapidly across all areas of the College, reaching 4,000 by 1975/76. As budgetary pressures increased, the College took a deliberate decision to redirect resources to the rising numbers of full-time students at the expense of the expanding evening programme and recreational courses. By 1977/78, the College welcomed a further 200 full-time students onto the campus at the expense of

752 evening students. The day population of the College was 1,000 (a mix of full-time and part-time) with slightly fewer part-time students than before as employers felt the impact of the economic recession. That year, total enrolments were only marginally improved on the levels of 1970/71 – some 3,200 students. As a consequence, most areas of the College saw a reduction in enrolments caused primarily by the reducing number of evening students.

With reductions in part-time staffing budgets and the impact of increased fees, all of which were designed to ease budgetary pressures, the role played by the College in the development of adult provision in the local community began to be undermined.

By the end of 1979/80 the total net expenditure for the College was 1,064,940.

Catchment Areas for Full-time Courses

By the mid seventies, the determination of student eligibility increased tension. Many areas of the College record a constant

battle with the newly formed Gwynedd Authority over discretionary awards for students, where students were deemed to be outside the College catchment area.

In 1978, the Gwynedd County Council forwarded a copy of the document *'Catchment areas for further education colleges in Gwynedd'* to Clwyd County Council. The document included catchment areas for Llandrillo Technical College, but was rejected by members of the Governing Body on two counts: they had not been included in any of the early discussions and the matter had already been discussed at the Further Education Sub Committee of Gwynedd County Council. After several deferments and with some reservation, the Clwyd Education Authority and the Governing Body finally agreed to observe the boundaries, where comparable courses were available and where the College's catchment area was defined as follows: *'The West boundary will be a line extending South from a point midway between Llanfairfechan and Penmaenmawr to a point North of the Lledr valley and thus to include the whole of the*

Conwy Valley and the Lledr Valley, the boundary to continue South Westwards until it meets the Meirionnydd District boundary.'

Despite the constraints imposed by Gwynedd, boundaries began to take on a new meaning with the long awaited announcement of the new multimillion pound highway, the A55. Initially introduced with the Collcon Report of 1968, this east-west expressway along the sea front not only addressed the congestion issues faced by most local areas in the College's immediate catchment area, it eventually paved the way for college expansion to a much wider catchment area further east.

The A55 sweeping along the coast.

The Impact of Budgetary Controls

On 21st May 1976, the *North Wales Weekly News* reported, *'Would-be students turned away'*. At the time of reporting, over 880 applications had been received for only 350 available places.

In his first Annual Report, Mr Sparrow boldly stated: *'We will have to adjust our attitudes to a new situation in which the efficient use of limited resources will involve turning away qualified applicants for college places in increasing numbers.'*

By 1977, the College was entering a phase where even greater financial control on both capital and revenue resources meant that the College curriculum was becoming severely constrained. To address the situation, the Principal decided on the following approach:

1. He became a member of the meetings of Clwyd County Council, enabling him to speak on matters directly relating to the College and placing the College on an equal footing with the North East Wales Institute whose the Principal was already a member; and

2. Made determined representations about the future development of the College, in a supplementary report to his Annual Report 1976/77, at the meeting of the Governing Body in February 1978.

He reiterated the College's objectives as stated in Clwyd County Council's Position Statement:

• to provide facilities for further education in West Clwyd and East Gwynedd and, in certain specialist fields, for the whole of Clwyd and Gwynedd and also for other Authorities; and

• to provide in conjunction with Managing Agencies facilities for training and retraining adults and for training the young unemployed and students sponsored for Industrial Training Boards.

Would-be students turned away

MORE than 300 potential students will not be able to enrol for courses at Llandrillo Technical College, Colwyn Bay, when the term starts in September, because there are not enough places for them.

This was stated this week by Mr. W. G. Sparrow, principal-elect, who said that the College had already received 880 applications for the 550 places available on ther various courses, and more applications were expected.

This compared with 550 applications received at the same time last year.

There had been a particularly sharp increase in applications for the catering, secretarial, hairdressing and nursing courses, though some vacancies remain in the basic courses in science and technology.

Mr. Sparrow said: "There have been clear signs over the last two years that, in the absence of increased accommodation being made available for the college, we would reach a stage when a large number of well-qualified applicants for many of our courses would have to be turned away. That stage has now been reached.

It is most unfortunate that we are unable to meet the demand for further education for the young people of West Clwyd and East Gwynedd in a period of high unemployment. The prospect facing many of our school-leavers is a grim one indeed."

Report from the *North Wales Weekly News*, 21st May 1976.

He asked how, in the absence of any future Development Plan, the College could meet the demand for places and fulfil these objectives. The most recent building programme had simply eased the overcrowding that existed, which meant quite simply that there was no room for growth in the future.

With the continuing budget restrictions, Clwyd County Council encouraged their colleges to develop only those courses that were self-financing; this effectively steered colleges towards Advanced Level work and cost recovery courses at the expense of the craft-related courses. The Principal, Mr Sparrow was unequivocal: *'It is an accountant's answer not that of the educationalist.'* With continuing youth unemployment and the potential to create a vacuum in vital areas of craft training for young people, the College was clear it would resist such actions and continue to rationalise and develop cost-effective further education provision in the absence of any additional building programme. In essence, option (b) of his report was adopted: *'... to reduce the number of students accepted to allow for a civilised atmosphere and effective learning conditions within the college.'*

A further issue was that 23% of the teaching work in 1977/78 was undertaken by part-time staff. Whilst this provided a great deal of flexibility and specialism, it was a problem for the full-time staff who were required to absorb the non-teaching components of the part-timers' work on top of their already heavy burdens. The Principal was concerned and reminded his Governing Body that invariably such pressures would lead to a declining quality profile. The areas most significantly affected were the Commerce & Liberal Studies Department and the Engineering, Construction & Science Department.

A major report on teacher education and training, The James Report of 1972, recommended a broader role for the higher education colleges, and the White Paper, *Education: A Framework for Expansion*, promoted diversification and rationalisation. With the dip in the birth rate resulting in fewer children in the schools, the government announced a halving of the number of student teachers in 1973. It also became clear that the government intended to increase the proportion of student teachers trained through the one year Postgraduate Certificate in Education (PGCE). The implications for the College of such a high cohort of part-time staffing were to become quite significant.

In May 1978, after discussions regarding the implications of the Health & Safety Act, the Administrative Committee of the Board resolved that a College Safety Committee and a post of Safety Officer be established with effect from 1st September 1978. The post was to be from the teaching staff of the College with five hours' remission. Health & Safety was to become a major consideration for the future.

By 1979/80 the College employed 104 full-time lecturers, 90 part-time lecturers, 14 administrative staff and 85 support staff.

Administration

Faced with the increasing non-teaching welfare requirements of the rising student numbers and the introduction of many new different educational returns, pressure on the administration of the College grew. Income from sales was increasing, telephone lines were inadequate, returns were becoming varied and complex and staffing levels were too low. This together with poor accommodation heightened a growing problem. The pressure was relieved to some extent with the new administrative building programme in 1978 and the addition of several new posts over the decade including a secretary for the Principal, a Safety Officer and a Nurse. A new telephone exchange also alleviated pressure as it enabled a speedier response to callers who were growing impatient over waiting times.

The College Departments continued to request additional administrative support to help with the increasing volume and demands of paperwork resulting from the increased number of students and the complexity of the differently funded student

A representative sample of the College administrative staff and student support staff including the College Registrar (also known as the Senior Administrative Officer), one of only three positions in the College which was appointed directly by the Governors of the College. The three positions included the Principal, Deputy Principal and Senior Administrative Officer.

programmes. It is hard to imagine the pressures on staff in a generation where the old 'banda' copiers were the principal source of reproduction. Throughout the seventies, however, their repeated requests for full-time clerical assistance remained unanswered.

Accommodation

The building programme of the late sixties which had faced continued deferment,

The land nicknamed 'the rustics works' transferred to the College in 1974.

finally made an entrance in 1971, when agreement was reached for the erection of a new student hostel and a new motor vehicle workshop in time for 1972. In January 1974, the College also gained two/three additional teaching spaces and additional car parking spaces from the 'rustic works', an area of privately owned land adjacent to the College site at the roadside, which was finally bought by the Denbighshire Authority in 1972 and transferred to the College.

A further addition to the teaching stock was five demountable units, transferred from the newly built Ysgol Bryn Elian. Sadly the 'mobile' became a much deplored but preferred solution to building extensions in the cash-strapped eighties resulting in increasing numbers each year.

By 1975, however, the College was beginning to feel the strain. The changing pattern of education and training programmes for a student population of all ages and from a wide range of educational and social backgrounds provided a challenge when set within the context of limited resources. The continued failure to implement the proposed College building programme meant a shortage of adequate and suitable teaching and communal space. Each year, departments attempted to manage their timetabling more effectively through the introduction of twilight sessions, staggered lunchtimes and extended teaching hours.

In the Principal's report of 1974/75 he states: *'... the teaching accommodation that does exist is used with a degree of efficiency which gives rise to space occupancy levels which few colleges could match.'*

During the second half of the seventies, after years of continued pressure from staff and governors alike, and with the newspaper headline reporting that students were being turned away in large numbers, a flurry of building works from the rolling building programme were finally approved and started. In 1976, the Administration/ Teaching block was approved at a cost of £166,000 and by April 1977, the Department of Education and Science agreed to provide £80,000 to finance the new food preparation and service kitchen

Some of the 26 mobiles acquired by the College over the first three decades.

which was to become known as 'Starters' Restaurant'. There were no windows in the restaurant, a consequence, it is said, of its location directly opposite the female hostel! The new teaching block provided eleven additional teaching rooms (classrooms and laboratories), a new student common room and an audio visual aids room.

Despite such good news, not everyone in the College was pleased with the announcements. Full-time students, upset over losing their common room for two terms during the building programme, staged a protest march through Colwyn Bay to the Civic Centre where they put their case to the Mayor of Colwyn Bay and the Chief Executive. They then marched back to college where they staged a 'sit-in' in the classrooms in protest. The newspapers were quick to record the discontent, despite the fact that the action was short-lived and that everything was back to normal two days later.

The new Administration area was completed on time in readiness for the September 1978 start, followed quickly by the Teaching area in November 1978. Mr Sparrow, whilst feeling the strain of the upheaval, stated in his Annual Report of 1977/78: '... *as a building programme was in progress we were encouraged to battle on by the fact that there appeared to be some light at the end of the tunnel.*' His comments however were tempered with the statement that despite such additions, the College was now desperate for additional teaching support areas.

By September 1979, not only were the new catering extensions in place but work had commenced on a new classroom/staff workroom block, a unit for students with learning disabilities and a single storey library block at the end of the teaching block. A further five classrooms were added to the teaching stock, providing the extra capacity needed to accommodate the additional students supported by the new library which housed 50,000 books, a private study area and small tutorial rooms. This flurry of building works may have provided some relief to a college in desperate need of teaching space, but did little to appease the owner of the Rhos-on-

The one-storey library block.

sea golf course next door. He threatened legal action against the Denbighshire Authority if they did not address the drainage systems of the College before any more building works were undertaken. Rainfall from the roofs of the many new buildings, coupled with inadequate drainage on the College site had already created flooding which added to the drainage issues of the golf course. (For the record, this matter was addressed and resolved although in 2001, the College once again faced major flooding following freak weather conditions.)

Students and lodgings

The hostel, opened officially by Mr Van Straabenzee, Under Secretary of State for Education, on 20th October 1973, catered for 60 female students. It was a long awaited development but typically, within a few years of opening, was considered ten years too late – students' attitudes to round-the-clock supervision had changed! Despite the small number of students involved, their impact on the College was quite significant. The

The hostel, opened in 1972.

girls required the services of a full-time matron, Miss Ellis. The refectory opened for evening meals and the library was required to extend its opening hours. College cleaning services were extended as was greater security from the College support teams. The hostel, therefore, was expensive and only just covered its costs adding to the pressures on the college at a time of financial shortfalls.

By the mid-seventies, the College had 600 full-time students, with 250 or 42% placed in lodgings. For some this meant five days a week; for others it was seven days. The majority were on hairdressing or catering courses that drew students from across North Wales. Approximately 60% of the students requiring lodgings were female. The welfare section was responsible for arranging safe lodgings, with the majority residing in houses and the remainder in flats. Each year this became more difficult as the local population changed its attitudes to student boarders. By 1973/74, despite the opening of the hostel, the accommodation situation was acute, with students wanting greater freedom and some landlords finding the rents simply insufficient to cover the costs of the students.

In 1978, 33 Malaysian students aged 17 to 19 joined the ranks of the student lodgers. The students, studying A levels with the intention of gaining places at English universities, were being sponsored by the Malaysian Government with a view to returning home as qualified engineers to work for their Government. They were all placed locally and fitted in well with the student population. One issue, however, that became a concern was the lack of religious facilities locally. Students had to travel to Liverpool to attend prayers in the mosque until the Malaysian Government stepped in and provided a mobile classroom which was temporarily converted into a makeshift mosque.

The responsibility for the students' welfare fell to the part-time Student Accommodation & Welfare Officer. This post remained part-time, despite a threefold increase in the student population during the decade.

The Student Association

In 1978, the Students' Association fell foul of the Principal and the Vice Principal. *The Pioneer* newspaper, held an exclusive interview with the Vice Principal, Mr Brown, over the students' decision to publish a 'Rag Mag' which was 'too blue'. The Principal had written the foreword encouraging local people to give generously without knowing the content, and he was embarrassed to find that many of the jokes used were regarded as offensive by some readers. The position was defended by the magazine's editor who claimed the magazine was not intended to be a child's comic and had already been vetted by the police before publishing. The controversy did not dampen spirits and the Rag Week ended well, raising over £650 for local charities and the local hospital radio.

The following year, the students' Rag Committee went ahead once again with the publishing without any College vetting. In an attempt to forestall antagonism, the compilers wrote – '**To our critics** ...*We apologise in advance if you are displeased or offended but if the contents of any rag magazine did not cater for the tastes of the majority of its readers it would never sell ...*'

The Rag Parade also faced difficulties that year as it became a victim of the lorry drivers' strike. Only two lorries were spared for the Parade, which meant some 250-300 students had to improvise. Bikes, cars and students on foot made their way to Eirias Park where the Mayor of Colwyn Bay presented a bottle of wine to the winning float, *Alice in Wonderland*.

Students dress as punk rockers, babies and girls from St Trinian's in October 1978 to raise money for Muscular Dystrophy Week.

The College Academic Structure in 1979

**Department of Business
& Liberal Studies**
Mr T.T. Richards
Deputy: Mr R.H. Pritchard

Business Studies, Management, Liberal Studies

**Department of Engineering,
Construction & Science**
Mr A Hill
Deputy: Mr B.G Dutton

Engineering, Motor Vehicle, Construction, Science

Department of Fashion & Health
Mrs M.L. Halliwell
Deputy: Mr R.W. Davies

*Health Studies, Hairdressing, Art, Home Economics,
Recreational Activities, Beauty Therapy*

**Department of Hotel Keeping
& Catering**
Mr N.J. Russell
Deputy: Mr M. Bates

*Food Preparation, Food & Beverage, Food Service,
Accommodation Operations*

Department of Secretarial Studies
Mr E. Busby

The New Departments

**Commerce & Liberal Studies
Department**—The decade finished with
this major Department being split into two
new Departments: the Business & Liberal
Studies Department and the Secretarial
Studies Department. In November 1977,
the restructuring was discussed at the
Administrative Committee, following a
report by the Principal about the heavy
volume of work and the need to separate
out the Office Studies section. This
change was recommended and formally
approved by the Governing Body in
December 1977, revising the College's
departmental structure created in 1969
from four departments to five. For
reporting purposes, this summary shows
the two Departments operating as one,
although strictly speaking, the two became
independent at the start of the academic
session 1978/79.

The end of the decade saw a consolidation
of full-time/day-release student numbers
but a reduced number of evening students,
a result of the imposition of the severe

financial constraints and cutbacks in part-time lecturer expenditure. Total enrolments of 1,044 in 1979/80 represented a significant growth on 1969/70 levels but a lower number than those at the middle point of the seventies when enrolments topped 1,200. Numbers continued to fall as evening classes felt the strain of the budgetary cuts until 1982/83, when the College began to grow once again.

Despite this reducing trend, the decade saw many changes to the curriculum with new courses introduced and old ones removed. By 1974/75, following the raising of the school leaving age, the once traditional two year course in commercial studies was phased out, to leave only one year clerical and secretarial courses.

Losses were replaced with gains elsewhere. During the early years there had been a steady boost to full-time enrolments with the introduction of the Secretarial (post A level) course. In 1974/75, some 54 students were recruited to this one year programme which more than compensated for the demise of the commercial studies courses. Another change was the growth in TOPS courses sponsored by the MSC. These altered each year: one year a 27 week programme in shorthand/typewriting, two back to back 18 week clerk/typing courses the next year.

This decade also saw the demise of the old ONC and OND programmes to be replaced in 1978/79 with the new BEC General and National Diplomas across many of the Departments within the College. New curriculum had always been a challenge, and whilst the General Diploma results were initially encouraging, only eight of the twenty five students passed the 1st year National Diploma, failing primarily on the statistics module. The matter was quickly remedied with an enhanced hour of teaching each week.

Accommodation remained a problem with around eighteen classes to cover each hour of the working day. As the Department had only nine classrooms, many groups were taught in the refectory or in hired premises at Penrhyn New Hall, almost one mile away. By 1974/75, three of the

Young police cadets are taught English, law, first-aid, lifesaving and sociology before they join the force.

modules meant the system was woefully inadequate. Urgent replacement was needed by the end of the seventies at a cost of £7,000.

Engineering, Construction & Science Department—Enrolments increased steadily during the seventies particularly within Science where a one year, full-time foundation programme comprising O levels and a two year, full-time programme of A levels had been introduced. An additional 100 full-time students were added to the Department's enrolments by 1979/80 only to be offset overall by the removal of the pre-apprenticeship courses in Engineering, a direct consequence of the raising of the school leaving age.

demountable units were in use within the Commerce & Liberal Studies Department.

Another major issue was in the computer area. The first two terminals were introduced in 1972/73 linked to the ICL 1900 computer at the then Flintshire College. These were replaced by the SWTP 6800 microprocessor which was only a four user system. Demand from the industry and the BEC students for the Computer Studies/Data Processing

By the end of the decade, Engineering, Construction & Science was arguably the second largest of the five departments with 825 enrolments, slightly higher than those recorded in the Department of Fashion & Health. However, as the Department of Fashion & Health was without the benefit of any recorded enrolments for its physical education and servicing, its numbers in real terms were actually greater than those in Engineering, Construction & Science!

Part-time day enrolments also increased across the Engineering, Construction and Motor Vehicle sections, despite the loss of the gas fitting courses from the Wales Gas Board who had transferred all training to Llandaff in Cardiff in 1971/72. Like Commerce & Liberal Studies, the Department responded by introducing new programmes which included six link courses for ROSLA students across all engineering and construction disciplines.

The introduction of the motor vehicle (RTITB) workshop in 1972, provided much needed space for Motor Vehicle although the area continued to struggle with inadequate workshop areas. A plan for rationalisation of the workshops was submitted to the County Architect during 1972/73. The plan, over a period of four years, was intended to create separate areas for each of the Engineering, Construction and Motor Vehicle Sections. Despite issues of health and safety, noise

and overcrowding, the financial provision was continually removed from the budget each year until 1978, when the College building programme created a new electrical technology room, a new science laboratory and a motor vehicle-related laboratory and significant rationalisation of space throughout the College as a whole.

Notorious for resolving their own difficulties, the gas fitting workshop was converted by staff to create an electrical laboratory after the gas courses were withdrawn. Whilst the intention was well meaning, the development was severely criticised by the County Architect's Department which authorised trades people to rewire the area immediately.

Always working faster than the official systems controlling them, new courses were being introduced at all levels to cater for demand. On many occasions, courses were started before being officially authorised. One example was the Mechanical Engineering Part II course, started in September 1972 and 'halted' later the same year when a directive to cease immediately was issued by the Welsh Education Office, as no approval had been obtained and inadequate facilities existed. Undeterred, the Governing Body did not give up, citing employers' support and new equipment to persuade the Welsh Education Office to keep the course going. Student enrolments grew steadily throughout the seventies, and most rapidly after 1975, with the introduction of the foundation courses and increased support from the Training Boards to help the unemployed. In this traditionally male dominated profession, it was not until 1978 that the first female student won a place on the EITB course for electricians.

By 1979/80, the Department, like the Commerce & Liberal Studies Department was moving into the computer age and running the first courses in industrial applications of microprocessors.

Department of Fashion & Health—
With the reorganisation of 1969/70, Fashion & Health initially became one of the largest departments in terms of enrolments and one of the most varied in terms of curriculum. The area was responsible for Hairdressing, Health, Domestic Subjects, Art and Physical Education. During the seventies, the number of enrolments rose to a high of 1,371 in 1975/76, falling to 800 enrolments in 1979/80, a consequence of the decision to reduce evening classes with the budgetary cuts. Of these 800 enrolments, the Department had some 230 full-time students, 150 part-time day students and over 400 evening students. In addition, and without the benefit of the enrolments, the Physical Education section's servicing commitment to the College's full-time students was almost 50 hours each week.

Although accommodation remained a major issue throughout the seventies for all the areas, progress was incremental and solutions were generally found. However, only a Sports Hall would provide the long term solution to the lack of suitably-equipped accommodation for the Physical Education Section (later renamed Recreational Activities).

Hairdressing—In the early years, the Hairdressing Section witnessed significant growth in full-time numbers, primarily as a consequence of the introduction of beauty-related courses. The Annual Reports show how adaptations to existing rooms provided the alternative to new practical areas. For example, a new hairdressing salon was constructed out of the Board work classroom creating new space for an extension of programmes and the introduction of beauty therapy and men's hairdressing. By 1977/78, a beauty salon (without the solarium and sauna) was in full operation with a second salon being prepared for facials etc.. Staggered lunches were also introduced to provide a further 10 hours' practical time to ensure that all student needs were met. The section saw the introduction of the WJEC hairdressing scheme and became assessors, for the first time, of their own students for practical subjects.

The Section introduced Link courses with the schools and TOPs courses on behalf

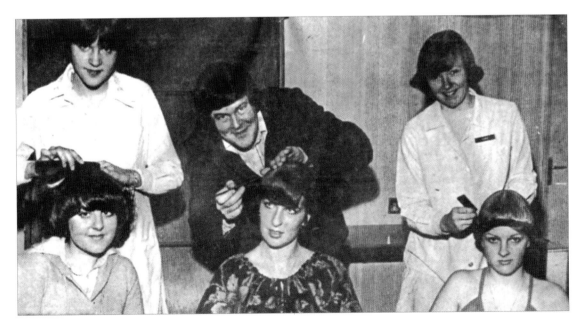

In 1978, three students made their way to London for the hairdressing finals.

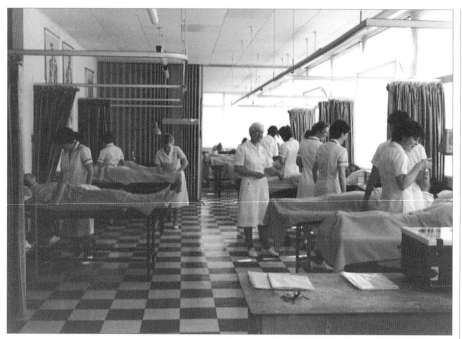

Full-time beauty students from the 1979 intake provide facials and massages for their clients in their newly prepared salons on 'C' corridor.

of the MSC, but struggled to introduce block-release courses as support from the industry for this style of course was very disappointing. In 1974/75 approval was given to run the CGLI (760) Advanced Course and by 1976/77, full-time courses in beauty therapy with hairdressing were being offered. In 1979/80, a programme of Industrial Release was introduced and all full-time students spent a week in local salons as part of their work experience. Results were generally good except for

the day-release results in 1976/77 – a consequence of overly keen employers and students attempting to gain qualifications in two years despite the required three year programme of study. The matter was corrected immediately!

The Section continued to have a presence externally, hosting the area final of the Association of Hairdressers' annual competition, providing support backstage with the wigs for a visit of the Welsh National Opera in Llandudno and supporting the catering students with hairdressing and beauty therapy sessions at the Rhos Abbey Hotel when Llandrillo students took over the running of the Hotel. In 1978, for the first time in the history of hairdressing at the College, three students won through to the finals of a national hairdressing competition in London.

Health—Numbers of full-time students increased in 1972/73, with the introduction of three streams of pre-nursing students, each graded and managed according to students' ability. Group 'C' comprised twelve 15 year old females who had not covered the CSE syllabus and left school early. Despite initial concerns about their capability, almost all of them passed their first year training and successfully entered nurse training at the end of their programme.

The Section continued to introduce new courses, most of which were part-time. This included the Diploma in Nursing, the Playgroup course, dental surgery assistants and a programme of community care for the cadets of the North Wales Police Authority.

Placements were still a major feature of the different courses and pleasingly, the relationship between the College and the local hospitals continued to build in strength.

In the early seventies, the area did gain a practical room with a bed and trolley – a major triumph as previously, much time had been wasted setting up at the start of each class before teaching could begin. In 1974, the College appointed a nurse which relieved many of the Health lecturers from leaving their classrooms to attend to students and staff in the College sick room.

Physical Education—This area must be commended for its ability to continue to support and provide recreational activities for students and staff alike despite having had no real suitable accommodation. Each year's Annual Report pleads with its readers for a new sports hall whilst gallantly presenting another option to engage its students in various activities.

As part of the full-time curriculum, all students were required to undertake one hour of recreational activity. This area therefore had to service this demand, equating to around 50 hours' teaching each week. The requirement was a challenge and, coupled with a student population that was growing in age and taste, necessitated considerable thought about the curriculum on offer. Twilight and evening courses tended to revolve around folk dancing and ladies' and men's keep fit, with the later additions of yoga and golf, choral singing and guitar classes. Numbers varied each year but there was a noticeable downward trend in 1979/80, twilight and evening recreational activities having all but disappeared.

Mr Griffiths presenting a shield to netball players just before his retirement.

Early in the seventies, the Academic Board approved a scheme to hire outside premises on a regular basis. Several options were introduced, including the twilight option of the keep fit for men in the then Colwyn High School, dry slope skiing, albeit fee paying, at the Mountaineering Centre at Plas y Brenin, swimming in the new pool in Llandudno, riding at a local riding school and playing tennis at Penrhyn New Hall. The students were generally enthusiastic and, pleasingly, the new options were successful in their early years.

Outdoors, as the emphasis moved away from major team games, there was a corresponding reduction in the number of pitches required. By 1972/73, the second soccer pitch was no longer in use and the rugby pitch was converted into two five-a-side pitches. College clubs reduced in number with only the Table Tennis club representing the College competitively. Despite the limited involvement externally, the College introduced various internal competitions, including netball, indoor football, five-a-side and badminton, which attracted between 150-250 students each year. They would accumulate points for their performances at different events, resulting in a declaration of the winners at the annual prize-giving ceremony.

The area continually introduced new courses on a regular basis; some never recruited sufficient numbers but others, like the new Link Course in modern educational dance at CSE Mode III level, was buoyant for several years before numbers fell off. The nine hole golf course on the playing fields was in full use by 1974/75 and popular with many of the older students.

The Department of Hotel Keeping & Catering

The Department of Hotel Keeping & Catering—continued to grow in size with enrolments exceeding 525 by the end of the seventies, matched by a doubling in staff numbers. The area was buoyant and from the records we can see that staff and students alike were highly engaged in practical work both in and out of the College. On average, the Department hosted at least five banquets a year including the prestigious Epicurean. In 1973, the area hosted the luncheon for the Under Secretary of State for Education as he opened the new hostel and in 1974, students provided afternoon tea for members of the new Clwyd Authority.

The seventies saw the growth of the HND, albeit with one very worrying fall in student enrolments in 1973/74, hastily corrected the following year with increased publicity. Enrolments in the craft courses also grew and it is clear from the records that both full-time and evening programmes increased steadily. As full-time students hit 200, the Department reaffirmed their requirement for additional teaching space and a dedicated hotel reception area. In 1974, the HND was reviewed by HM Inspectors who made clear recommendations for improvement.

By the mid-seventies, new course development slowed simply because space was restricted. Like other departments, it staggered lunches and extended the working day to 19.30 in an attempt to provide quality teaching and practical space for the enrolled students. Having so many students in one restaurant tested the lecturers both in terms of supervision and being able to find everyone jobs to do. Not

The Duck Press, part of the silver collection from the Llandudno School of Hotel & Catering.

Margaret Thatcher's speech to the Welsh Conservatives

"On the evening of 26th November 1976, Tory Leader Margaret Thatcher addressed her party workers in the old hall at Llandrillo College. The *Western Mail* reported that she had attacked the Labour Government for making 'a bad job of ruling Britain'.

At 4.15 p.m. the students left College and at 4.45 p.m. Mrs Thatcher and her party, quietly and securely, entered the buildings.

Few actually witnessed the event that evening because of the strict security although it is known that caviar on small pieces of toast was one item on the buffet served by staff and students: a snippet of knowledge from those who enjoyed a few samples as they were en-route to the hall!"

only did inadequate teaching space become a major issue, so too did the need for more storage areas, staff rooms and changing facilities. Providing a suitable storage area for the college silver was also becoming a major challenge!

In March 1977, the Academic Board reported that the College had accepted £86,000 for extensions to the Catering Department and the reorganisation of the Home Management area. This was completed in time for the 1979/80 academic year at a cost of £118,000. By 1977, the opening of the restaurant in the evening was hailed as a major success, with themed overseas evenings providing training for the third year HND students.

The Department was regularly involved in external competitions and most annual reports record students' successes. In 1971, the College won the Alfred Bostock Memorial Book Prize for bakery and during 1972/73, the bakery students achieved six out of the first nine places in the Hovis Area competitions in Chester. In 1974/75, the students worked alongside the Wales Tourist Board to design meals under the 'Taste of Wales' campaign.

In February 1978, supported by Hairdressing and Beauty students, the Department took over the operations of the Rhos Abbey Hotel for the weekend. Twenty five guests, each paying £25 for the entire weekend, were treated to Welsh culinary delights devised by the students and entertained with dancers, a harpist and a comedian. The students took on the roles of cooks, cleaners, waiters, porters and Hotel Manager, whilst students from Fashion & Health provided a range of hair and beauty treatments. The weekend was so unique that a local newspaper sent one of their reporters undercover to report on the experiment – which she hailed as a great success. The hotel 'take-over' became an important training event thereafter for many years.

By the end of the decade, the College, with its new facilities, evolving organisational structures and improving responsiveness to the local economy was beginning to operate in a way which reflected its growing confidence and its position as an emerging college on the North Wales coast. Historically, the focus of educational provision had always been clearly defined: the North East with Wrexham and the North West with Bangor. As the decade came to a close, the role of Llandrillo was beginning to assume a new strategic importance which was eventually to challenge the domination of the more established educational centres in North Wales.

The Rhos Abbey Hotel.

An evening of culinary delights as students serve a medieval-style banquet to the guests at the Rhos Abbey Hotel.

7. The Eighties – Valuing Educational Provision

An aerial view of the College taken in the late sixties.

The eighties continued the acceleration of change and culminated in some of the most profound and far-reaching developments to occur within further education. In 1988, the Education Reform Act introduced a new scheme of delegation for further education colleges which brought greater autonomy and the introduction of student driven formula funding which was to quantitatively relate the size of the College budget to student programmes.

Mr W.G. Sparrow retires after 13 years service as Principal.

These proposals were greeted with enthusiasm by the further education colleges but before we learn how they impacted upon the future development of the College, it is important to record the many other significant changes that were taking place throughout this decade as a consequence of the internal and external environment. These included the transfer, in 1987, of college ownership to Clwyd County Council, plans for a new tertiary system across the whole of Clwyd and the announcement that the Manpower Services Commission would become responsible for 25% of college business.

Looking back at the eighties, it might be said that the changes occurring were simply preparing the College for its new future. To the credit of the staff, the changes were embraced enthusiastically and it is clear that the ground shifted significantly as new foundations were being laid to prepare the College for its new role, where satisfying clients' demands became very much part of the new mission.

The decade ended with the retirement of the Principal, Geoff Sparrow, and the appointment of Huw Evans who, at the age of just 39 years, was one of the youngest Principals in the UK when he joined the College team in August 1989.

Student Enrolments

The 1980/81 academic session was one of consolidation, continuing the pattern of the previous three years of reduced enrolments after the frantic growth experienced during the mid-seventies. Total enrolments stood at 3,000 with a very different profile of students as a result of the decision to redirect valuable resources from evening to full-time provision. Full-time numbers stood at 909 in 1980, an increase of 74% on the 1970 level of 522.

Despite some early indications of growth, the Principal reported in 1983/84 that enrolments were once again at a standstill, reflecting the static supply of resources – quite simply, the College was full.

Although there was no major 'teaching' building programme during the late eighties, there were ongoing adaptations to existing buildings. The long-awaited Sports Centre created new space as did extensions to the workshops. A very unusual twist also occurred in 1987 when college ownership transferred to Clwyd County Council. As the Gwynedd students were redirected to study in Gwynedd colleges, space no longer required for residences was released in the hostel, providing much-needed room for staff accommodation. However, most demands for new quality accommodation went unanswered and the rising number of students just had to be content with more mobiles for additional classroom space.

By 1986/87, student numbers were once again on the increase, particularly in Business Studies and Secretarial Studies where computer technology was beginning to have a major and long-lasting impact on new course provision. In contrast, Departmental Annual Reports record that commercial courses were no longer being developed. For every new development there was a cost, and the limited consumable budgets were needed to provide essential teaching aids for the full-time and part-time students. As the number of computers increased, so did the need for storage disks, ribbons, paper etc.. As the school links programme increased so too did the demand for a consumables budget.

Each department faced its own challenge in keeping full-time provision adequately resourced, so it is not surprising to read that commercial courses were perhaps seen as just one step too far. The lecturers' 'work to rule' towards the end of the eighties also added to the slowdown in the development of new and additional course provision.

Royal Visitors to the area

On October 28th 1981, the Prince and Princess of Wales visited Caernarfon; to the scene of his Investiture twelve years before. The Royal couple travelled from Rhyl, along the costal resorts to Llandudno where the Prince opened the new Aberconwy Conference Centre. The Department of Hotel Keeping and Catering had received an invitation from Aberconwy Borough Council to provide a luncheon buffet for the opening of the Centre to welcome the royal visitors.

The Daily Post newspaper recorded *'Both made do with a light snack, Princess Diana with a small piece of salmon in aspic, and Prince Charles with the same followed by a request for some Stilton and Caerphilly. They refused any sweets…..but the Princess walked across to the students to congratulate them on their cooking'.*

By 1988/89, as Mr Sparrow's era drew to a close, student numbers had more than doubled and exceeded 6,400 (1,800 FTE).

Mode of attendance	'79/'80	'83/'84	'86/'87	'88/'89
Full-time	909	997	1257	1351
Part-time	736	1021	1042	1086
Evening	1580	1681	2168	3991
TOTAL	**3225**	**3699**	**4667**	**6428**

After the first year of the new Principal in 1989/90, the eighties closed for business with almost 7,500 students (2,265 FTE).

Budgetary Issues

The actual net budgetary position for the College in 1979/80 was £1,066,228. By 1980/81, this had risen to £1,424,890, rising again in 1981/82 to £1,715,500. In real terms, this seemingly large increase was a result of inflationary increases, which meant that additional expenditure was always at the expense of savings or increased income. In the revised budget for 1980/81, for example, the microprocessing equipment was purchased from savings arising from the outworkings of the organisational study on the administrative areas of the College.

By 1984/85, the net budget stood at £2,412,890 of which Gwynedd County Council was now being asked to find almost £1 million. At the Governors' meeting in November 1983, Gwynedd asked for the College to reduce its expenditure by 2%, a cut which was imposed the following year.

The mid-eighties was a time when European Social Fund (ESF) monies began to flow into colleges so it is disappointing to record that the success of a major bid for Hotel Keeping & Catering to meet the challenges of the 21st Century, in partnership with the LEA, ultimately failed because Clwyd did not provide the match funding needed – a situation not dissimilar to that in the Secretarial Studies Department, where plans for spending ESF monies were also halted.

One very positive note, however, was that after many years of waiting, the departments finally received dedicated secretarial assistance.

At the close of the decade, the estimated net expenditure for 1989/90 was set at £2,705,800, representing no more than a modest inflationary rise on '84/85 levels.

Accommodation

With the building programme of the late seventies and the addition of many mobile classrooms, the College teaching spaces increased in number. Few regarded this additional space as an improvement; it was simply '... *tacked on to the existing building and then shared out*'. The decision to increase the number of full-time students at the expense of the evening students coupled with increasing numbers of day-release MSC-funded students and School Links pupils continued the pressure on accommodation.

In 1980, the long awaited Sports Centre was approved subject to the completion of a circular road around the College and the installation of a new ring main to improve the power supply to the many additional areas which had been constructed since 1964. Some additional car parking spaces had been provided, but for the first time, the issue of car parking became a serious problem with the need for at least a further 100 spaces. The shortfall was so great that evening students were parking on both sides of Llandudno Road creating traffic and safety problems.

The absence of a major programme to resolve the problem of additional, quality teaching space meant that the departments could only grow at the expense of each other. In 1982/83, discussions were once again under way to consider the provision of a new teaching block to accommodate and relocate two departments and allow the others to rationalise the space vacated. In November 1983, the proposal was submitted for inclusion in the Building Programme 1985/86. In the meantime, the Business & Liberal Studies Department was using Penrhyn Church Hall three days a week, Penrhyn New Hall two and a half days a week and the Teachers' Centre in Colwyn Bay on three days a week.

On another positive note, the library had settled into its new location at the end of

'D' block and by 1983, all full-time students received an induction programme on the facilities available. Although the intention was to open in the evening, staffing levels struggled to support working after 5.30.

Also in 1983, the rationalisation of the motor vehicle, engineering and fabrication workshops was underway. The RTITB motor vehicle workshop was extended to enable all mechanical engineering, machine and fitting work to be housed together, with all motor vehicle work carried out in the main workshop and fabrication/plumbing taking place in the existing EITB workshop.

Non-teaching space was also becoming problematic. The refectory was too small and queues stretched down the corridor despite the introduction of staggered lunchtimes. As more and more students gathered on the corridors, the demands for additional cleaning services became necessary and litter became a major issue. A student common room, capable of providing for the growing student body, was clearly long overdue.

Work on the Sports Centre commenced in the spring of 1983, opening in September 1985. This brought with it a long-awaited snack bar with 84 seats, a kitchen, shop and stores. Food was transferred from the refectory daily and the snack bar remained open in the evening, facilitated by the use of two vending machines. The pressure on the refectory began to ease as students used the snack bar in the Sports Centre.

The Sports Centre.

By the mid-eighties, 47% of full-time students were living away from home. These included students from Malaysia, the Commonwealth and the EEC. Liaisons between the College and the landladies were helped by the annual landladies' luncheon which helped to maintain good working relationships. Despite a threefold increase in work, the College still operated with a part-time Accommodation/Welfare Officer.

During the summer months, the hostel was opened to members of the public seeking residential accommodation. French, Danish and Italian students added to the takings in the summer as did students from Deeside High School who stayed at the hostel for a week's holiday each year. In addition, the cricket team from Barnsley and, in 1983/84, the Ladies Golf Union booked the hostel and meals for a week for their international competitions.

In May 1988, following the Resident Steward's retirement, the Board approved the demolition of his bungalow. In the meantime, the bungalow was used as a Staff Development Centre pending the

The Resident Steward's bungalow up for sale.

erection of the new Painting & Decorating workshop in 1989.

Little by way of major building work was undertaken during this period, although committee minutes do show that small scale projects, adaptations and constant reorganisation alleviated in part the annual demands for space. The main hall, which saw many changes of use during the lifetime of the College, was once again facing change in 1989. In the search for even more additional teaching space, the stage was removed and a new teaching area created.

MSC and Private Training Providers

The Manpower Services Commission (MSC), instigated as a political response to rising unemployment in the seventies, expanded its remit further with the *New Training Initiative* (1981). This extended the work of the MSC to include coordination and management of the Youth Training Scheme (YTS), formerly YOPs and the Technical & Vocational Education Initiative (TVEI) which was to be managed by Local Authorities.

YTS funding was allocated directly to training providers, who included not only the further education colleges but also employers providing work-based training and private training organisations. This control over educational funding and the policy of funding private training providers directly was perceived as a threat by many in the further education sector, which had hitherto seen itself as the main, if not sole provider of 'off the job' training.

For recording purposes, the students were treated differently, requiring separate paperwork and monitoring information which added to the workload of staff already stretched to meet the requirements of the FEFCW funded students.

Private training organisations became active in the catchment area of the College quickly and relied heavily on the College's facilities to provide 'off the job' training. Whilst initially posing no threat, by the mid-eighties this changed and the College faced competition for students as providers created their own training facilities.

In September 1983, the North Wales Youth Training Agency (NWYTA) was established as a 500 placement agency. Of the College's YTS enrolments most were funded directly from the NWYTA allocation. Using third party funding made planning difficult and when this was added to the constant changes in the YTS scheme itself, the College faced a difficult period in sustaining a viable MSC student base. One significant example occurred in 1984, when the MSC announced that the introduction of a two year placement scheme, approved for 1986, was to be delayed by two years.

For those placed on the BTEC National Certificate in Business Studies, about to start their second year of studies, the College simply picked up the costs from their already limited budget.

As the area's main training provider, NWYTA began to provide their own 'off the job' training especially in the fields where specialist equipment was not essential. By the end of 1985, they had established their own training wing on the Quinton Hazell site in Mochdre where specialist workshops, classrooms and a hairdressing salon were equipped. This led to the withdrawal of the business studies and hairdressing provision traditionally provided by the College.

In terms of employer engagement, the College recognised the need for a planned approach to providing day-release courses for an increasing number of school leavers entering the YOPs/YTS schemes. Not only did it enable the College to keep a careful eye on valuable resources, it brought stronger links with industry, the careers service, the MSC and the schools. It also became clear that the concept of an academic year was becoming blurred, with new employer-driven courses being required to start throughout the year.

Predicting future demands became more difficult under the National Training Initiative (NTI). It soon became clear that the lack of specialist space could not be resolved merely by increasing the number of mobile classrooms – the College had been provided with a further 8 mobiles during 1982/83 to meet additional accommodation demands. Whilst this form of sub-standard accommodation affected full-time students in particular, it also restricted the development of the NTI day-release programmes. In many cases,

Waitresses, receptionists, porters and a barmaid from Llandudno and Colwyn Bay learned how to become more customer focused and make the most of their jobs on a Government sponsored 15 week course organised by the Hotel & Catering Industry Training Board.

new course provision for the NTI was determined, not on demand, but on the number of existing students on any given day of the week.

Disappointingly, the College did not succeed in securing its own training contract until the end of the decade.

Technical & Vocational Education Initiative

The Technical & Vocational Education Initiative (TVEI) was announced in 1982 and Clwyd LEA was selected to host a pilot scheme in 1983, with the intention and money for the scheme to run for five years. The emphasis was based upon consortia/collaboration and required the LEAs to take a key role as managers of the TVEI projects. The aims of TVEI were to complement the national curriculum and ensure that the education of 14-18 year olds provided young people with learning opportunities which would equip them for the demands of working life in a rapidly changing society. This included:

- Relating the curriculum to the world of work;
- Providing knowledge, competencies and qualifications to work within a highly technological society as part of the world economy;
- Providing work experience;
- Solving problems, working in teams etc.;
- Having access to advice and guidance.

For many, this initiative brought together local schools and colleges in exciting curricular developments, but for all the effort afforded most projects gained little by way of permanent national recognition. Despite the introduction of varied and flexible provision, much of TVEI was by way of knowledge-based qualifications as opposed to performance-based assessments and the concepts of credit accumulation and transfer.

That said, the College, together with eight schools in Clwyd and Gwynedd, must be commended for their work in instigating six vocational areas which would assist students in obtaining employment. During 1984/85, some 52 lecturers/teachers became involved in a training programme which involved two meetings each week of the year, seven co-ordination meetings and evaluation sessions, making it one of the largest pilots planned. The scheme was considered impressive nationally not only because of its size but also because of its geographical spread and the fact that it dealt with issues relating to bilingualism.

In July 1986, the TVEI extension was announced which was intended to give all 14-18 year olds access to a wider and richer curriculum based on the lessons emerging from the pilots. Later in September 1986, two courses were identified as being TVEI: the C & G 481 in Recreation and Leisure Studies and the BTEC ND in Computer Studies which attracted funding for enhancement and innovation. By October 1986, the College had appointed a TVEI Co-ordinator to work on the TVEI extension project (TVEI/E) which was to commence funding in September 1988. This in turn was to be followed by a five year funded development programme in September 1990.

One further development relating to TVEI was TRIST (TVEI-related In-Service Training). Clwyd LEA secured £300,000 for this development, from which the College successfully secured funds and a new post of co-ordinator for in-house training programmes.

Certificate of Pre-Vocational Education

Partnership working was becoming the norm, as was the consensus that the education of young people from 14 onwards should be seen as an on-going and integrated process, which should not be disrupted by change from one institution to another. In 1980/81, a School/College Liaison Committee was established with representation from Head Teachers, College Principals and Officers of the two local authorities. Their first task was to plan new collaborative ventures in an era of a diminishing school population. This included the teaching of computer studies for pupils of local secondary schools and the development of a City & Guilds foundation course at Ysgol Emrys ap Iwan.

By 1982/83, the school link programme included every secondary school in the catchment area of the College, particularly in the General Diploma Courses.

By 1984, this programme was being replaced by the CPVE scheme – an educational qualification for students over 16 in schools and colleges who wanted a one-year course of preparation for work or further vocational study. The College became the only one in Wales participating in the pilot programme for the CPVE scheme, piloting business studies provision.

By 1984/85, there were 236 students in total attending the College one day a week which had risen to almost 500 from 13 different schools by the close of the decade.

Training Initiative Unit

In 1982, the College created the new Training Initiative Unit to oversee, organise and promote all MSC-related projects within the College. By the end of 1983, the Unit was generously staffed with three lecturers on remitted time, a full-time secretary and two clerical assistants responsible for 41 courses with 455 trainees across the College on mode A or mode B programmes.

The College had hoped to become a managing agent directly but this did not materialise and instead, they found themselves seeking business as the service providers for the appointed Managing Agents, which included NWYTA.

Despite this setback, in the first year income generated was approximately £0.5 million, with the Unit operating from the main College site and an outreach site in Denbigh High School with three classrooms.

The Unit continued throughout the eighties until 1988, when falling YTS numbers led to a review and the emphasis shifted to developing commercial short courses. The Unit became known as the Industrial Liaison Unit, supported by an Advisory Committee chaired initially by the Head of Department of Engineering, Construction & Science and later by the Vice Principal, Dr Bibby. By 1988, staffing levels had been reduced to two, the Unit Manager supported by a part-time secretary only.

Initially, short course provision was the sole remit of the renamed Unit but as the decade closed, the Unit became involved in other projects including the first major submission under the European Social Fund (ESF) and a partnership bid with Clwyd County Council to be included in the County's Integrated Development Operation (IDO) submission to Brussels.

The Unit was responsible for managing the College database of local companies to support the marketing of the Unit. With a very determined focus on providing courses to support local industry, the Unit became involved in many different ventures including bespoke courses for BS 5750, a drop-in centre for local businesses, distance learning to support the rural areas and the 'Three Counties Colleges Consortium', a partnership of 13 colleges in Clwyd, Gwynedd and Powys promoting cooperation.

'… The catering trade sets its stall out. Students from the College provide cookery demonstrations at the 22nd Welsh Catering Trades Exhibition in Llandudno in 1983. Mr David Williams, exhibition organiser for the Llandudno Hotels and Restaurants Association was delighted with the response, despite the economic recession.' (*Weekly News,* 26 January 1983)

In September 1989, the Unit was included in the 'Window on North Wales' Exhibition at the Aberconwy Centre which proved extremely beneficial for the College and local businesses. In the two and a half years of operation to September 1990, the Unit organised 176 short course/consultancies and made a profit of some £70,000.

Operating within a College environment was sometimes tiresome as the Unit could not respond as quickly as liked to the requests and demands from business. As the new Principal took position so did his plans for the future; the removal of the Unit to be replaced by a private limited company. By the end of 1990, a College Company – Bay Enterprises (Wales) Ltd – was set up by way of a Charitable Trust to provide the flexibility required.

Work-related Non-Advanced Further Education

Since its inception in 1974, the MSC had been negotiating with Local Authorities and colleges for the supply of different types of training courses. The White Paper of 1984, *Training for Jobs*, brought new responsibilities: to provide support for vocational education and training which was geared to the informed needs of the labour market. Claiming that the FE Sector had been insufficiently responsive to the needs of employers, the Government had decided to transfer resources to the MSC from the rate support grant settlement. To ensure compliance, the MSC were given the power to purchase, or control, 25% of work-related FE.

Planning for work-related non-advanced further education (WRNAFE) became an important new driver for colleges. Based on a three year rolling development plan between the Local Authority, the MSC and the College, the plan was to be reviewed annually and produced in sufficient detail to ensure the College successfully appropriated a meaningful annual financial contribution to its delivery. The first development plan related to the three academic years commencing in 1986/87.

A further development in the mid-eighties was the emphasis placed by the MSC on women returning to the secretarial workforce. Two twelve hour, fifteen week bespoke courses were introduced in 1986 aimed at updating skills using the new technologies and building confidence to assist with job seeking and interviews. These were just the first of many courses, spread across the local communities.

For those who care to remember, the MSC was absorbed into the Department of Employment in 1988 and renamed, first as the Training Commission and then as the Training Agency. In 1991, most of its functions were taken over by the Training and Enterprise Councils.

Other Curriculum Changes

By the mid-eighties, so many course structures had changed, that issues with the curriculum became a main agenda item at the course team meetings. The merger of the Business and Technical Education Council (BTEC) provision made it important for Departments to start working together on submissions. The introduction of the NVQ (National Vocational Qualification) in 1986 came with similar issues and was to have a major impact on staff training and delivery techniques.

Cross-college staff development, therefore, became essential as the move towards integrated curricula continued. The newly appointed Staff Development Officer was instrumental in managing the Local Education Authorities' Training Grants (LEATGS) and securing funds through initiatives like TRIST, developing both formal and informal In-Service Training (INSET) programmes to keep staff abreast of change. The LEATGS budget, set at non-advanced level, was for teaching staff only. In 1988/89, the College received almost £30,000 which provided 150 INSET events over 648 days to 160 members of staff. No allocation was made for advanced work, as the total advanced allocation was awarded to NEWI – a decision which caused much disquiet among College staff. Non-teaching staff had only the main College budget for training support.

Staff from the Department of Fashion & Health participate in a series of team-building activities including canoeing, climbing and camping.

Changes were also occurring in the structure of GCE Advanced Level (A level) courses, GCE Ordinary Level (O level) and Certificate of Secondary Education (CSE) courses. The AS (Advanced Supplementary) examinations were introduced by the Government to provide students with 'half subjects' at the same standard as A level subjects; the intention was to allow students to spread their studies across a broader range of subjects. The General Certificate of Secondary Education (GCSE) also replaced GCE O levels and CSEs. There was criticism

from schools, colleges and LEAs about the lead-in times to bring about change, although securing £2,000 to assist with the changeover to GCE did help the College to introduce the GCE in English Language in time for 1986. Noticeably the take-up of AS subjects was much slower.

During 1988/89, the Secretarial Department evaluated the implications of the NVQ and its effect on the work of the Department. Introduced in 1986, by the specially formed NCVQ (National Council for Vocational Qualifications), the NVQ was not just a qualification but a system of learning and accreditation. An extensive staff development programme was undertaken to look at the restructuring of curriculum delivery in order to create a competency-based workshop environment for the students concerned. Decisions were taken that year to extend the NVQ into a large proportion of the work of the Department in time for the academic year 1989/90.

Partnerships

During the eighties, curriculum development centred on partnerships including B/TEC, NEWI (formerly the North Wales Institute), employers and the Local Authorities. In the year 1982/83, the Business & Liberal Studies Department, in conjunction with NEWI and the Police Authority, developed a BEC Higher National Certificate in Public Administration (Police). Developed in a record time of six weeks, the first students commenced their studies in 1983/84, thanks to the hard work and cooperation of all those involved.

Another joint venture with NEWI was the development of the HNC in Motor Vehicle Studies, as part of the Open Learning scheme. By September 1985, four members of staff had embarked upon writing material for the Open Learning B/TEC units. One year later, they were complete and Motor Vehicle was able to offer the units to the C & G Full Technological Certificate students to enable them to convert their qualification to the HNC. By 1987, a new full-time HNC in Motor Engineering and Management was in place.

Also in Motor Vehicle, a consortium was formed for the specific purpose of purchasing £11,000 worth of microelectronic motor vehicle instructional equipment. The Department of Trade and Industry gave £3,400, the remainder being found by the College and local employers.

In 1981/82, the Engineering Department resumed an overseas programme with the Malaysian Government which enabled students to study GCE Courses. This lasted until 1983/84 with the College being one of three praised for their consistently good results; the other two being Blackpool and Kingston. Undeterred by the completion of this programme, the scheme was extended to Hong Kong and Nigeria.

Another partnership venture included the opening of a microelectronics training workshop on the College campus, as part of the Clwyd Information Technology Centre. This workshop, which was to operate independently of the College, was both an educational venture and a commercial venture, where the products developed were marketed and sold. In 1982/83, ten trainees started in the workshop and were instructed in the basic skills of electronics assembly and testing, amongst a host of additional subjects. The 'Purple Palace', as it became known in the nineties, was the first of many flexible workshops across the College.

Students with disabilities finally gained access to the second floor of the College in 1981, with the help of a new interior lift. Alterations costing £30,000 provided the new lift and ramps near the refectory and library blocks.

Special Needs Unit

Another important development in the early eighties was the development of the Special Needs Unit for students with learning difficulties and physical disabilities. In 1982/83, ten students enrolled on a two year full-time programme which was designed to ensure that no student with a special need spent more than 50% of their College week solely within the Unit. In essence, students were required to play a part in college life and establish themselves as part of the student body. In December 1982, a new and eighth Advisory Committee was created – the Special Needs Advisory Committee, whose first meeting was held in February 1983.

Of the first ten students, three students required accommodation so partnership arrangements were made with Ysgol y Gogarth, Llandudno, to provide the specialist accommodation required for the students to be able to study at the College. By 1983/84, the ten students had started their second year and a new cohort of ten students began their programme – making a total of 20 students. That same year, the Unit introduced a school link programme involving four local schools which grew continually throughout the eighties.

By September 1985, the Unit had introduced a full-time transition (bridging) course and a one-day-a-week course for groups of disabled adults. Work experience was an important component of the full-time course, and for many students, progression was made possible with further education and training as part of the YTS schemes.

With the introduction of the Unit, greater attention was given to issues of access. There was restricted access to some parts of the College because doors were not wide enough or corridors were too narrow, and only single storey buildings met the requirements of some students. In 1985/86, a lift to all three floors of the main block was installed but disappointingly the top floor of the newly built Sports Centre remained inaccessible until the end of the decade.

In 1988/89, with help from All Wales Strategy funding, the College established a gardening area with a greenhouse to the rear of the site to allow students with severe learning difficulties to learn gardening skills as a vocational/leisure activity. Although the first year consisted

The students of 2004 display their produce in the greenhouses, erected during the eighties.

primarily of constructing the garden area, some plants matured and were sold across the College.

The development of the Unit was to lay the foundations of what was to become one of the most successful units in Wales, providing a much-needed local resource.

Computer Technology

Many microcomputer systems were installed in the College between 1980 and 1985, financed from a variety of different funding sources, including the two Local Authorities who were happy to provide computers which would support the School Links programmes.

By 1983/84, the College's computer provision had improved considerably. Each year saw an improvement on the one before, with each Department generally requisitioning their own computer purchases, bidding wherever possible to improve on their numbers. In 1984, the Engineers introduced 6 nimbus research computers for CAD/CAM use, and in 1985 and 1986, the Secretarial Department changed the use of two of their typewriter rooms to house 32 ferranti computers.

Secretarial courses were immediately oversubscribed as the 'electronic office' and keyboarding courses attracted wide interest from the community. Despite new technology introduced each year, replacing outdated equipment was generally slow in relation to the total stock held. In 1986/87, the impact of outdated equipment was felt by the Secretarial Department which faced pupils transferring from electronic typewriters in the schools to manual ones in the College. No consideration had been given to the impact on the College when Clwyd purchased 30 electronic typewriters for each high school using a LEA-TVEI funded programme. Despite this oversight and the constant limitations on new capital growth, students were not deterred from attending the typewriting courses, which resulted in overall enrolments rising quickly to 600 over the two years, an increase of some 45%.

Maintenance was a cross-college function undertaken by the College technician who battled with servicing and repairing the many different types of computer as well as the inadequate electricity supplies! The speed and reliability of the Business & Liberal Studies Department's network of computers was constantly affected by the electricity supply when other users logged on within the College or when someone switched the kettle on in the staff room – something staff were most indignant about until a new source was supplied in 1985.

In 1988, the School of Catering suffered their own blow to modernisation and computerisation; the County Council were unable to match fund a significant bid from Europe which meant £180,000 of new computer equipment was lost to the area.

By the end of the eighties, the College had invested in a new administrative system which would assist with the increasing complexities of student data. In 1988/ 89, the Fretwell Downing Computerised Management Information System, or CMIS as it became known, was introduced. As the College moved towards greater autonomy, this system became the main source of management data for the annual budgetary allocation.

The early years of CMIS, however, were challenging and statistical reporting at the end of the eighties appears to have lost its ease of reporting student numbers as the programmes became more funding driven. In his first Annual Report, the new Principal made it clear that CMIS was a necessity and that it would need significant staffing and associated staff development in the future.

In 1990, the electronics workshop moved out to a double mobile to alleviate the pressure on accommodation. Clearly visible with its bright shade of purple, the 'Purple Palace' became a truly flexible drop-in-centre for students, one of the first of its kind.

The Audit Commission

In 1982, the Government created the Audit Commission which was seen by many as the culmination of increasing central government influence over local authority financial practices. By June 1985, the Audit Commission had published 'Obtaining better value from Further Education' which became the subject of a prolonged attack by the media suggesting Further Education was falling short in terms of cost-effectiveness. Although the Audit Commission faced a barrage of challenges to its methodology and conclusions, the report did provide the College with the ammunition it had waited for to review the actual position in terms of the College's finances and practices, something that for years had been the subject of much debate.

The first area of concern was the fact that early calculations, based on the 1984/85 statistics, reported a £320,000 shortfall in the College budget. Based on a net expenditure of £2,552,419 and 1,494 Full-time Equivalent Students (FTEs), the cost per student at Llandrillo was calculated at £1,708 compared to a national average of £1,900.

The second area that caused the Governing Body concern was the calculations used in determining the non-teaching staff in the College. The shortfall was a staggering total of 27.5 staff, which made up an estimated £220,000 of the shortfall calculated. The request over many years for clerical assistance in the Departments was now beginning to be justified.

The Principal, Mr Sparrow reacted fiercely: *'Some people have resented the fact that I have described the College as being 'run on the cheap'. I repeat the charge and call in evidence the Audit Commission report.'*

By 1986/87, the Governing Body had commissioned the County Treasurer's Department of Clwyd County Council and members of the Education Department to undertake a comparative unit costing exercise. The result of this exercise produced findings – treated with a degree of caution – as follows:

Unit costs per course per FTE students	
Llandrillo	National Median
£1,513	£2,178

Statistically, this could be stated as showing Llandrillo Technical College to be underfunded by 31% or in monetary terms by £1,093,260 (i.e. 1644 FTE x £665) – a major triumph for the College but a matter of concern for the Local Authority.

Local Authority Governance

During this period of financial review and during the 1985/86 academic session, a number of other decisions were also taken which were to have a major impact upon the College:

1. The decision by the Clwyd and Gwynedd Authorities that as from April 1987 the College would be governed by Clwyd alone. The change meant that total financial responsibility would lie with Clwyd County Council, with Gwynedd County Council charged extra district fees (out county fees) for their students. All assets and liabilities were transferred to the ownership of Clwyd County Council. (It is recorded that Gwynedd gained financially from the arrangement, certainly in the early years of transfer and ultimately longer term as students from Gwynedd were encouraged to study in the Gwynedd Colleges. It is no coincidence that these changes occurred simultaneously with the Bangor Normal College transferring to Gwynedd County Council, having previously been managed under the aegis of the North Wales Counties Joint Education Committee.)

2. The suggestion that the Clwyd LEA would be recommending the establishment of a new Tertiary College in North West Clwyd.

3. Recognition (at last) that there should be an examination of cost-effectiveness and resource allocation in Further Education by Clwyd Education Authority. This would later confirm the situation that the College was indeed underfunded.

4. The intervention of the MSC in the planning of Work-Related Non-Advanced Further Education (WRNAFE), as recorded above.

College Administration
January 1982

Senior Administrative Officer
Mr D.G. Waller
(who went on to become Clerk to the Corporation)

Administrative Staff
Mr B.P. Davies
Mrs O. Davies
Mrs M.E Hughes
Mrs J.B. Lawson
Mrs I. Williams

Library staff
Mr R.D. Horton
Mrs M. King

Hostel
Miss E.O. Ellis
Miss C.K. Jones

Catering Manager
Mr S.N.E. Watson

College Nurse
Mrs E.W. Betts

Accommodation & Welfare Officer
Mrs M.B. Bates

The first three decisions were related in that a single administering authority made it easier to focus on secondary/tertiary reorganisation and critically review resource allocation in the process.

College Management

The College management structure had not changed since the late seventies when the Departments increased to five. The Board had three standing committees: the Staffing Committee, the Administrative Committee and the Disciplinary Committee. These were supported by the Academic Board which comprised 16 teaching and 2 non-teaching staff and the Health & Safety Committee.

There was one change to the senior personnel of the College. In 1982, the Vice Principal, Mr J.A.K. Brown left his post and was succeeded by Dr A. Bibby.

The Administrative Committee was essentially the Senior Management Team responsible for the day-to-day management of the College. With the acceleration of change and the announcement of a likely move to a tertiary system, considerable attention was now being given to reorganisation and the need to redress the rigid departmental structure which was in place. Whilst the structure had served the College for well over 20 years, both management and the Board could see the growing importance of enhancing cross-college developments.

At the Academic Board meeting of 10th December 1986, a subcommittee of five members was formed to investigate and report on the concept of a single site tertiary college to be based at Llandrillo. A full report on 'Going Tertiary' presented to the Academic Board in June 1987 contained the findings of the subcommittee and essentially presented the case for supporting a new tertiary build on the Llandrillo Technical College site: '... it is in essence a tertiary college in embryo.' On a scenario building exercise, the report was clear that a single site college with an increase of 1,000 full-time students needed an additional 50 classrooms at a capital cost of some £3-4 million. At the time of the inspection in October 1987, no major decisions about reorganisation had been taken for fear that a revised structure at this time might be short-lived once the tertiary proposals were announced.

Full College Inspection 1987

In the Autumn Term of 1987, the whole College was inspected by HM Inspectors. A short 10 page report had been prepared to provide the Inspectors with background information, including a summary of the key operational areas and the original objectives of the College as set out in section 6:

1. To provide facilities for further education in West Clwyd and East Gwynedd and, in certain specialist fields, for the whole of Clwyd and Gwynedd and also for other Authorities; and
2. To provide, in conjunction with Managing Agencies, facilities for training and retraining adults and for training the young unemployed and students sponsored for Industrial Training Boards.

In contrast, the Inspection Report issued in January 1988 by the HMI was 54 pages in length. The conclusions however were brief, the more detailed comments being found in the body of the report. Some of the key findings detailed in the conclusion were as follows:

1. The College offered a wide range of course provision.
2. The growth in College provision had not been matched by investment in equipment and accommodation and the College was operating beyond the capacity of its resources.
3. Examination results were generally satisfactory.
4. Approaches to learning were any of the following three statements: exemplary, well planned or not well planned at all. (A very simplistic statement for a concluding remark!)
5. Curriculum management needed addressing within agreed aims and priorities.

The conduct of the inspection, spread over two and a half weeks, and headed by a

In 1982, Dr A. Bibby became Vice Principal following Mr J.A.K. Brown's resignation from the post to relocate to Canada.

General Inspector who had been attached to the College for a number of years, was met with some disquiet. The Inspectorate team remained at arm's length; some Inspectors did not even meet the Principal or Vice Principal. Feedback sessions were not standard and on several occasions the

The College hits back – Report from the *Daily Post* on Wednesday 12th October 1988

College blast for top level 'critics'

by Carl Butler

A HIGHLY critical HMI report on Llandrillo Technical College at Colwyn Bay was "littered with inaccuracies," the college principal claimed yesterday.

Concerned councillors even considered completely rejecting the report, while others said it should be deferred until its author was prepared to answer questions.

Principal Mr Geoffrey Sparrow revealed at a Clwyd education sub-committee that he had raised his concern with HM Inspectorate and two representatives were travelling to Clwyd for discussions on the report in December.

"It undermines the value of the report when it is so shot through with inaccuracies," Mr Sparrow told councillors.

Former head teacher Coun Fred Jeavons said some of the comments in the report were "damning and awful allegations."

In its conclusions, the report – following an inspection last autumn – says: "The college is operating beyond capacity. The management system does not permit the development of corporate policy. Staff roles are not well defined," among many other criticisms."

Coun Alf Jones said the authority should not respond to such an inaccurate document: "The senior HMI should be here to answer our criticisms," he said.

Mr Sparrow said the damaging statements had already appeared in the local Press. He said he wanted officials of the education department to be present during the meeting with the HMI.

Councillors agreed they would respond to the HMI report, refuting many of its criticisms as the Governors had already done.

Principal and key senior staff were not invited to attend. The Chairman and the Vice Chairman of the Governing Body were granted an opportunity to receive a verbal preliminary report over lunch but it was without the presence of the Principal. His formal invitation was at the meeting of the Governing Body when the General Inspector spent 55 minutes giving a verbal preview of the report to follow. The apparently haphazard arrangements of many of the inspection procedures meant that fundamental misunderstandings and generalised statements used to describe situations or facts were not addressed and could only be challenged once the report had been issued.

And challenged they were. The Principal, Mr Sparrow, responded to each and every numbered paragraph of the report, highlighting inaccuracies, poorly written sections and misleading statements. Of particular concern was the Inspectorate's disregard for the industrial action by teaching staff which had resulted in some pro-forma not being completed – the report simply declared it incomplete without any reference to the sanctions imposed on staff by their trade union.

Secondary/Tertiary Reorganisation

In July 1985, the Education Committee of Clwyd County Council requested a report on how the Authority was to cope with the reduction in the number of secondary school pupils in the order of 25-30% by 1990. The Director of Education reported that money had been removed from the rate support grant settlement which meant that action was needed to rationalise and reorganise secondary/tertiary education in Clwyd with the potential removal of schools' sixth form provision.

In December 1986, Clwyd County Council received the LEA's outline proposals on Secondary/Tertiary Reorganisation and agreed to a secondment of a full-time member of staff, so that preparatory work for the consultation process could commence with governing bodies, teachers and parents. The findings of the consultation were reported back to the Education Committee in November 1987.

The early recommendations were to have four Tertiary campuses; one on the NEWI/Plas Coch/Yale site; one at the NEWI/Deeside site; a third grouping Welsh Medium provision; and one either at Llandrillo or a twinned campus linking the College with Ysgol Emrys ap Iwan.

At the Governing Body meeting in September 1987, drawing from the recommendations of the report presented in June 1987, the Board unanimously agreed that the Tertiary College for North West Clwyd should be established on one site at Llandrillo. This was reported to the Education Committee who recorded that they had received a high quality detailed report which was clear in its findings: '... *The College Governors are in favour of tertiary reorganisation on a one site basis.*'

In June 1988, the Board were advised that difficulties still existed in the east of the county which involved the potential disaggregation of NEWI. The delay in securing agreement meant that the programme was always in danger of being rescheduled to a later date, but few thought that a delay would ultimately end in the project being scrapped.

1988 Education Reform Act

The Education Reform Act (ERA) received Royal Assent on 29th July 1988. The Act was primarily enabling legislation, the proposals becoming clearer as regulations, circulars and administrative memoranda were issued. Described as the biggest shakeup of state education since 1944, the Bill, prior to receiving Royal Assent, had faced a chorus of disapproval from all but the FE Sector and the CBI whose new Director General, John Banham, believed the changes were badly needed.

This Act was to have a significant impact on College development in the following ways:

1. The requirements for a smaller Governing Body with enhanced representation from industry and commerce. (The new Governing Body was introduced late in 1989, with its new powers effective from 1st April 1990.)

2. The introduction of formula funding for budgetary purposes, also effective from 1st April 1990, which quantitatively related student taught hours to the College budget. (Since under-resourcing had been a major theme of Mr Sparrow's Annual Reports, the hope was that the new budgetary systems would finally restore the College to a correct and adequate level of funding.)

3. A new scheme of delegation from the Clwyd Authority enabling the College to become more autonomous.

The New Governing Body

The first challenge for the Institution was therefore to introduce a new Governing Body with new powers as decreed by the ERA and to appoint a new Principal, following Mr Sparrow's announcement in December 1988 of his intention to retire. As with any changeover, procedures were delayed and for most of 1989/90, the Board operated without a signed copy of the articles. This made decision-making somewhat tortuous.

The final meeting of the 'old' Governing Body was held in April 1989, and is remembered not least because their final task was to appoint the new Principal.

Mr Geoff Sparrow's successor was Mr Huw Evans, Vice Principal of Pontypool College and former Head of Department at Bradford and Ilkley College. Like his two predecessors before him, Mr Evans was also a native of North Pembrokeshire.

After some thirteen years as Principal, during a period of unprecedented change, the legacy Mr Sparrow left behind was one of continued student growth, of steely determination to provide the College with the resources and the respect it required and, above all, recognition by Clwyd County Council that the College was indeed underfunded. In the summer of 1989, as the College poised itself for its new Principal, it did so in the knowledge that its curriculum base was sufficiently robust, its confidence was high and the budgetary shortfall had been identified and could potentially be rectified.

The inaugural meeting of the 'new' Governing Body took place in December 1989; Mr Glyn Catley was appointed Chair and Mrs Doris Griffiths Vice Chair.

Four Governing Body Committees were created: the Finance & General Purposes Committee, the Staffing Committee, the Health & Safety Committee and the Disciplinary Committee. In addition, the College Consultative Committees were approved as follows:

- Motor Vehicle
- Engineering
- Construction
- Health & Caring
- Hotel Keeping & Catering
- Leisure & Tourism
- Business Studies
- Secretarial Studies
- Special Needs

Under the Education Reform Act, the Governing Body was given increased powers and responsibilities. In order that they fully understood the new remit of operation, a programme of training was

Appointed in 1989, Huw Evans became the youngest Principal in Wales.

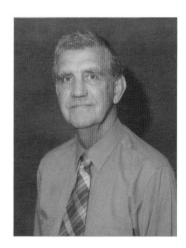

Mr Glyn Catley, appointed Chair of the College in 1989.

essential. Two training programmes were offered: a Clwyd LEA-led programme during 1990 and a workshop at the Further Education Staff College at Blagdon, Bristol.

College Restructuring

The focus of the late eighties/early nineties was on internal restructuring to meet the needs of an autonomous institution and the demands of tertiary reorganisation. Huw Evans, Principal, whilst admitting that '... *it is with some trepidation that any new Principal decides to modify and change the operation of a smooth running institution*', embarked upon a series of immediate developments to meet the challenges of autonomy, whilst sustaining growth and prosperity for the Institution.

His challenges, sent to all staff by way of a memo, were seen as:
• Transition to a tertiary college;
• Combating demographic decline;
• Increasing responsiveness to client demand;
• The development of a sense of corporatism;

• Working effectively and efficiently within a scheme of delegation.

The Autumn Term of 1989 therefore was a busy one. For the first time, the College had a mission statement. It was a mission statement that was to be linked closely with the newly introduced Annual Development Plan, outlining several broad objectives:

• **Quality**—achievement by measurement
• **Entitlement**—what students could expect
• **Comprehensiveness**—a wide range of opportunity
• **Progression**—entry and exit strategies
• **Access**—to under-represented groups
• **Responsiveness to Industry**— prioritising flexibility
• **Responsiveness to community**— removing barriers to entry and developing outreach centres.

It was also a time when the Structure Review Group established by the Academic Board produced an initial report on college restructuring. The changes brought about by the Education Reform Act and the move towards a tertiary system, not forgetting the aspirations of a new Principal, required a much greater cross-college dimension which was not seen as compatible with the departmental structure in operation. So whilst time was needed to consider the requirements of a new tertiary system, it was always clear to the Principal that any new structure could not wait for the considerable expansion which was likely under tertiary proposals at some point in the future. The intention was to restructure quickly, so that any new structure was sufficiently robust to ensure a smooth transition to a tertiary system as and when it finally happened.

College Structures

The Structure Review Group established by the Academic Board and chaired by the Vice Principal, Dr Bibby, produced its first report in December 1989. Initially working to full implementation by the 1991/92 academic year, the timetable was brought forward to 1st September 1990. Staff opinion agreed with this shorter lead-in time, as it was felt that uncertainty over a longer period would affect staff morale.

A review of the College curriculum had highlighted deficiencies in some areas. It was felt that Information Technology was underdeveloped and bilingual provision could best be described as limited. There were gaps in the areas of Performing Arts and Outdoor Recreation and there was an urgency to become more responsive to the community with the development of outreach centres. There was also a big drive to create greater 'student centredness' with increased flexibility in the way in which students learned and a desire to remedy the College's failure to become its own Managing Agency for MSC sponsored students.

In 1989/90, the Principal also faced his first curriculum challenge with the Higher Education sector: to retain and protect the HND Hotel Management and Catering course. Following a very successful campaign launched by the College, the Wales Advisory Board (WAB) agreed to preserve the course at the College.

The new structure was classified under two axes. The horizontal axis related to three key functional roles i.e. Finance & Administration, Client Services and Curriculum, each of which was headed by an Assistant Principal. The vertical axis related to the operational arm of the College, and comprised a further three Assistant Principals responsible for the Faculties of Business & Professional Services, Science & Technology and Tourism & the Arts. Each Faculty comprised four Schools of Study responsible for curriculum delivery.

The structure was designed to increase flexibility and responsiveness where success would be measured almost entirely on the degree to which the three Faculties and Schools of Study interacted effectively with the cross-college Functional Areas.

On 15th March 1990, the proposal for the College restructuring was approved by the Board whereupon the Principal announced his intention to appoint staff to key positions as soon as job descriptions were finalised in May 1990. Every existing member of staff was assigned to either a functional area or an operational area

FUNCTIONAL AREAS

Finance & Administration
– Mrs Gillian Ashworth
Client Services
– Mr Michael Wright
Curriculum Planning
– Mr John Carroll

FACULTY OF SCIENCE & TECHNOLOGY
– Mr Brian Dutton

Building & Civil Engineering
Automobile Engineering
Mechanical Production
& Electrical Engineering
Science & Maths

FACULTY OF BUSINESS & PROFESSIONAL SERVICES
– Mrs Barbara Russ

Business, Computing & IT
Business Studies
Secretarial & Office Technology
Health & Caring Studies

FACULTY OF TOURISM & THE ARTS
– Mr Michael Bates

Leisure & Tourism
Catering
Creative & Performing Arts
Humanities & Languages

Special Needs Unit

without any advertisement, posts being allocated internally according to existing work practices. New areas of work were advertised which included five new lecturing posts, one Marketing Officer and one Assistant Principal (Finance & Administration) who was appointed and in post by August 1990.

The appointment of Gillian Ashworth, a graduate Chartered Accountant, to the new Assistant Principal post was not general practice within the Further Education Sector. Indeed it was an early development within the Polytechnic sector which was seen by the new Principal as a necessary step forward in financial management as the College prepared for greater autonomy under the Education Reform Act. His foresight was to place the College in a very strong position with the announcement that colleges were to be fully incorporated in 1993. Indeed these early developments placed Llandrillo ahead of most colleges in Wales, and paved the way to capitalise on the new opportunities as and when they arrived.

Entering the nineties, the College was ready and poised to embrace the challenge of autonomy, introduce new and exciting curriculum developments, expand student numbers and gear itself up in readiness for the challenges of tertiary reorganisation.

It is fitting also to open the nineties with a celebration. On 26th April 1990, the staff of the College were invited to join an evening of cocktails, singing, dancing and food in a marquee in the grounds at Llandrillo to celebrate the 25th Anniversary of the College. The Summer Ball Committee, with the support of the BTEC Leisure & Catering students and the Principal, considered it right that everyone should celebrate 25 successful years of Llandrillo Technical College.

Gillian Ashworth (left), appointed in 1990 to the new post of Assistant Principal (Finance & Administration), the same Gillian who later became Gillian Evans, the author of this book.

INTO THE FUTURE WITH LLANDRILLO TECHNICAL COLLEGE

25

1965

1990

2015

JUBILEE CELEBRATION

LLANDRILLO JUBILEE CELEBRATION

on

18th May 1990
7 pm to 1 am

at

LLANDRILLO TECHNICAL COLLEGE

Ticket: £15.00.   Semi-formal dress

A staff invitation to the 25th Anniversary celebrations. The celebrations were an all day affair. The marquee was used to host a business/careers exhibition for prospective students by day and by night it played host to the sound of the Bro Aled Male Voice Choir from Llansannan, a three course carved buffet and a rhythm and blues band, 'The A Team'.

8. The Road to Independence

The nineties represented a significant watershed for the College. With change evident from his first few days in post, Huw Evans began his unrelenting drive to create one of the most successful colleges in the UK and bring about the changes needed to meet the needs of the local economy.

Working within the Education Reform Act 1988 and the imminent passing of the Further and Higher Education Act 1992, Mr Evans worked quickly to boost student numbers to ensure that the College could benefit from the newly emerging student-driven models of funding and reverse the patterns of underfunding from the local authority. Partnership working with schools, employers and voluntary organisations was a key component of widening participation and developing new learning opportunities for adult workers, women returners and young people who left school with few qualifications.

The College restructures again

The first Annual Report of the nineties – 1990/91 – was characterised by additional internal structure changes, building on those introduced in 1989. The flexibility that was fundamental to the newly formed college structure of 1989/90 was immediately tested when the Board approved the new Marketing Officer position at the level of Assistant Principal. This was quickly followed by a reorganisation of senior posts leading to a reduction in the number of senior

Mr Michael Bates and colleagues from the Catering Section at his retirement party.

managers, made possible by early retirements and staff successfully obtaining promotions externally.

Just one year later, the College had removed the tier of the Assistant Principals at Faculty level, created one further functional area at Assistant Principal level and added a new Curriculum Area: Community Studies. Responsibility for operational curriculum management was given directly to the Schools of Study/ Curriculum Areas.

With the promotion of two existing functional Assistant Principals to other colleges, the College welcomed three new appointments at Assistant Principal level, adding to the recently created position of Assistant Principal (Finance & Administration) and resulting in a very new senior management structure.

The Senior Management Team of the College included the Principal, the Vice Principal, Mr Bibby, and the four new Assistant Principals. Twelve Heads of Schools and the Heads of Community

---

FUNCTIONAL AREAS
Finance & Administration
– Mrs Gillian Ashworth
Human Resources
– Mr Gwyn Morris Edwards
Curriculum Planning
– Dr Tony Walker
Marketing & Clients
– Mr Glyn Jones

SCHOOLS OF STUDY
Building & Civil Engineering
– Mr A Carroll
Automobile Engineering
– Mr H Thomas
Mechanical Production & Electrical Engineering
– Mr G Barker
Science & Maths
– Ms R James
Business, Computing & IT
– Mrs S K Vaughan
Business & Professional Studies
– Mr A Pugh
Secretarial & Office Technology
– Mrs E J Cupitt
Leisure & Tourism
– Ms L Pixton
Creative & Performing Arts
– Mr G D'Isidoro
Hotel, Catering & Food Studies
– Mr S Patiar
Health & Caring Studies
– Mrs W P Coole
Languages and Humanities
– Mr P McAllister

OTHER CURRICULUM AREAS
Community Studies – Mrs N Dando
Special Needs Unit – Mr W Jones
College Company: Bay Enterprises (Wales) Ltd
– Mr R Gleave

Education and the Special Needs Unit reported directly to the Vice Principal as the Operations Team of the College. In all day-to-day matters, the functional areas liaised directly with the operational areas.

Education and Training for the 21st Century

In spring 1991, the Prime Minister, John Major, issued a White Paper entitled 'Education and Training for the 21st Century'. The message was clear: to improve and develop the education and training system for 16-19 year olds. This paper was to have a major impact upon the way in which colleges were run, taking the Education Reform Act 1988 to an even greater level of autonomy.

The overall aims included:
- to establish a framework of vocational qualifications;
- to promote equal esteem for academic and vocational qualifications;
- to extend the range of services offered by school sixth forms and colleges;
- to give Training and Education Councils more scope to promote employers' influence in education;
- to introduce the training credit;
- to promote links between schools and employers;
- to provide better advice and guidance about choices at 16;
- to provide opportunities for young people to reach higher levels of attainment;
- to give colleges more freedom to expand provision and respond more flexibly.

Item 9.2 of the section on *Better Colleges* stated: '... *Colleges lack the full freedom which we gave to the polytechnics and higher education colleges in 1989 to respond to the demands of students and of the labour market. The Government intends to legislate to remove all colleges of further education, which offer a minimum level of full-time or part-time day-release education, from local authority control.*'

Further & Higher Education Act 1992

The Further and Higher Education Act 1992 was the legislation that enabled colleges to take on full control of their affairs. Responsibility for funding and planning transferred from the local authorities to the Further Education Funding Council for Wales (FEFCW). The date of transfer was 1st April 1993, before which considerable work was needed to prepare for independence – or "incorporation" as it became known by college staff.

Towards the end of 1991, Touche Ross Management Consultants (Touche) were commissioned by the Welsh Office to provide a guidance manual on 'Getting Colleges Ready' in preparation for their release from local authority control. In May 1992, Touche organised a briefing for all Principals in Wales, one in Cardiff and one in Powys. The messages were lengthy but the summary was clear; unless you proved a state of readiness, there was no autonomy and no delegated funding.

Incorporation Project Team

Immediately after the Principal's briefing, the Board introduced a new subcommittee to deal with the implementation of the Act – the Incorporation Board supported by the Incorporation Project Team. The Team was coordinated by Dr Tony Walker; the Principal dealt with legal issues, the Vice Principal dealt with Estates, Gwyn Morris Edwards dealt with Personnel and Gillian Ashworth dealt with Finance and CMIS.

With the requirement to 'go live' on April 1st 1993, the College needed to secure the approval of their scheduled plans of implementation by summer 1992 and a full accounting system check by January 1993. The first year of operation was a 16 month financial year which changed accountability from the local authority year to the academic year.

Two key decisions were needed early in the planning framework to ensure staff and creditors got paid in April 1993. Unlike many other colleges in the sector who opted to remain with the local education authority as a provider of services, the College elected to break away immediately and make tendering for payroll and financial services a

The College changes its name as it prepares for a new era.

major priority. The new financial system adopted was a bespoke system called 'Dolphin' while the new payroll service was provided through an agency named 'Centrefile'. To support the two main systems, Barclays Bank was appointed to provide banking services. With the systems ready, the Team embarked upon the speedy transfer of paperwork from Clwyd County Council's Finance Department and Personnel Department. Whilst data was being loaded, preparations were in hand to customise the systems for College use. In 1989, the LEA had purchased the

Fretwell Downing (CMIS) Student Record software and by August 1992, a college wide network, using fibre optic cable, was installed. The CMIS software, together with the Dolphin system software, ran on dedicated file servers connected to some 60 PCs, forming the administrative network. The Management Information Systems (MIS) of the College therefore consisted of three separate systems; students, finance and personnel. With the longer term intention to acquire and integrate the different software, the system of student data collection via Fretwell Downing was seen as adequate to meet the requirements of Incorporation and the FEFCW.

By April 1993, the newly named college **'Coleg Llandrillo College'** was service ready with audit services and legal services in support.

Transfer of Assets and Liabilities

Running concurrently to getting the systems ready for Incorporation was the requirement to agree a schedule of assets and liabilities at the point of transfer and the surplus/deficit to be carried forward. Dr Bibby led the College Team working closely with the Education Assets Board (EAB) on what was to become a very prolonged dialogue with Clwyd County Council. The EAB appointed a caseworker to work directly with the College and Clwyd County Council to oversee the transfer process. By November 1992, the case worker was expressing concern that no proposals had been received from the local authority.

The transfer of assets not only needed a Schedule of Assets, it also needed a Condition Survey of properties and Equipment so that accurate valuations could be made for the College's opening balance sheet and ongoing future expenditure. In April 1993, the Building Conditions Report – which was to become known as the Hunter Report – established the condition of the buildings and the scale of capital expenditure required to ensure their adequacy and fitness for purpose. If the building required major capital works it was classified as Priority 1A, graded down to Priority 3 which meant works were necessary within five years. This document was to become the first of the Repair and Maintenance schedules of the College and one that was used for many years in determining allocations of repair and maintenance spending.

The Hunter Report was to become a matter of some disquiet in later years between the northern colleges and the southern colleges. The College's properties and equipment were valued at £1,392,144 inclusive of VAT and fees. Of the total, £703,641 was classed as Priority 1B – works of a less urgent nature. To the surprise of everyone, given the condition of many of the existing buildings, no works were deemed to be of a 1A status.

The Chief Executive of Clwyd County Council had assured the Principal that all relevant documents would be with the College by January 1993, although it was pointed out that transfer was not as straightforward as anticipated. Two issues were raised: firstly, the hostel was not recorded as belonging to the College and secondly, the land to the rear of the site had restrictive covenants which limited its

Extract
On 6th September 1995, the EAB wrote to the County Solicitor stating:
 'I cannot believe that it takes two months for anyone to agree with what I put in my letter of 3 July. This matter has been going on for so long it is just incredible ...'

use to that of a public utility. For nearly three years, the College battled with the County Solicitor of Clwyd County Council to agree upon the transfer of all the deeds relating to the College.

Several large case files are testament to the complexities involved in the transfer of assets and liabilities. In November 1995, hopes of a transfer were again dashed when the County Solicitor delayed transfer because of an unpaid invoice: an invoice in respect of income received for a reduction in the revaluation of rates in 1991/92. To add further insult to an already unpleasant situation and having proved that it was indeed the County Council that had benefited from the income, the College was left to shoulder the burden of an increased rateable value from 1992/93.

One final requirement of the transfer process was the need to prepare a schedule of 'shared properties', to ensure that no provision was interrupted after incorporation. In July 1995, this schedule showed that the Community team, alone, were recorded as working across 17 different venues. This represented considerable expansion given that the curriculum area of Community Studies was only formed in 1990. Many venues were local primary and secondary schools and libraries but in addition there were the more significant premises at:

• Tan y Fron Centre, Bylchau, near Denbigh
• Second Chance Centre, Rhyl
• Middle Lane Youth Centre, Denbigh
• Friendship Club, Colwyn Bay
• Nant Bwlch Yr Haearn Outdoor Centre

On 9th February 1996, the Principal was finally able to write to the EAB confirming that the process of transfer had been completed. In receipt of the college deeds, he thanked them '... *for their support over the last few years in what has proved to be a difficult process.*'

9. The Nineties – Education and Training Opportunities for All

The External Environment

Throughout its history, significant external changes have impacted upon the development of the College. The nineties are no exception, with two major changes to the funding regimes: the introduction of the Training and Enterprise Councils in 1990 and the newly created FEFCW in 1993.

Coping with two major funding reforms was challenging but changes in educational reform, which began again in earnest around 1995, meant that the full responsibilities of incorporated status began to impact, not only on the College management and staff, but on the College Board. Under the leadership of the Chair, Glyn Catley, and his Vice Chair, Malcolm Robbins, the College Board began to exert its authority and effectiveness as an employer and a key strategic organisation, providing the opportunity for the College to capitalise fully on its potential.

Although it is not the intention to burden the reader with too much educational detail, it is important to appreciate some of the external influences which impacted

Malcolm Robbins, Vice Chair of the College Board.

upon the College, its priorities and its educational ethos.

FEFCW and HEFCW

The Further Education Funding Council for Wales (FEFCW) and the Higher Education Funding Council for Wales (HEFCW) came into existence on 6 May 1992 and assumed full funding responsibilities for the two sectors from 1 April 1993. The Councils were responsible for securing the provision of further and higher education in Wales, funded directly by the Secretary of State for Wales and later in 1999 by the Welsh Assembly Government. Each Council was an independent body with its own Chairman but they were served by a joint management executive: the Welsh Funding Councils. The Councils were led by Professor John Andrews who provided the control and support for the evolving college sector.

The FEFCW was responsible for full and part-time further education provided in Wales; for encouraging the provision of vocational education; for promoting continuous improvement in the quality of further education; and for ensuring the development of provision for further education through the medium of Welsh. The FEFCW was also required to ensure value for money. The sector had a clear set of performance indicators, a common strategic planning framework, a robust quality assessment system and an information strategy to meet the needs of the College and the Sector. The FEFCW was given statutory responsibility for the Quality Inspection of Further Education Colleges and training organisations.

Relationships with the FEFCW were, in general, very good. There was open dialogue throughout their existence, which was extremely important in the early years as the College introduced the new funding systems, new student records systems (COVTECH), and processes of quality assurance and new contracts of employment for staff.

Heralded also as a watershed in the continuing development of the College by virtue of the speed by which it grasped the impact of ERA and the FHE Act 1992,

the College became well placed to respond quickly and positively to the national priorities as set out by the FEFCW.

During the early years of the FEFCW, colleges were encouraged to increase their student numbers, over and above funded targets, through a method of additional funding called the Demand Led Element (DLE). DLE, funded at 40% of the rate of unit funding, was initially unlimited and paid retrospectively. Student growth had already been earmarked as an essential component of autonomy post-LEA, so the College was well-placed to draw down DLE. At its peak in 1996/97, the College drew down an additional £450,000.

Importantly, additional growth was consolidated in the baseline figures for the calculation of funding the following year. The importance of accurate student projections was therefore paramount to effective financial planning, particularly as the increased income was important to the College's ambitions and aspirations in terms of buildings and equipment. The early preparations for independence paid dividends. Each year, the College budget increased by one million pounds and this provided the necessary funds to shape the modern College.

In 1997/98, the FEFCW replaced DLE with the Growth Incentive Fund (GIF). Unlike DLE, the GIF was a capped fund, and reward for over-achievement was related to only part of the College's activity. The financial impact to the College was significant, with GIF levels set at only one third of DLE levels. The introduction of GIF and the withdrawal of DLE in the same year meant that the years of compounded student growth came to an abrupt end.

By 1998, things were changing significantly and previously earmarked capital funding was consolidated within the overall budget allocation, leaving colleges to determine their own level of capital spending for the first time. Whilst this temporarily enhanced income levels for 1998/99, the management of capital expenditure became a very serious consideration each year.

FFORWM
(later called ColegauCymru)

In 1993, the newly incorporated Further Education colleges, recognising the need for a national body to represent their interests and work closely with the FEFCW, formed an organisation, known as 'Fforwm'. Chaired initially by Huw Evans, who had been instrumental in its formation, Fforwm persuaded the FEFCW to put in pump priming money of around £80,000 to enable it to become firmly established. This money was in fact top-sliced from the FE budget with the permission of the FE colleges in Wales. Fforwm, now ColegauCymru, represents colleges on a range of bodies and works closely with key decision-makers in Wales, including senior civil servants and Ministers as well as key organisations such as the Confederation of British Industry, the Federation of Small Businesses, the Welsh Local Government Association and Higher Education Wales.

Training and Enterprise Councils

In December 1988, a government White Paper entitled 'Employment for the 1990s' announced the abolition of the Manpower Services Commission (MSC) and its replacement by a set of local, employer-dominated bodies. In England and Wales these were called Training and Enterprise Councils (TECs) and in Scotland, Local Enterprise Companies (LECs), all of which were operational by November 1991.

The TECs took over all the training work that had previously been carried out by the MSC. The aim was to make training policy sensitive to local needs and impact on business growth.

The Training and Enterprise Councils were allocated budgets according to historical patterns. They also competed for other resources including the European Social Fund (ESF). In North Wales, the North East was serviced by 'NEWTEC' which became operational in September 1990 with a budget of £6.2 million. The North West was serviced by 'TARGED'

which became operational in February 1991 with a budget of £1.8 million.

Building on these initiatives, the 1991 Government White Paper 'Education and Training for the 21st Century' encouraged the development of skills through the notion of lifelong learning, enabling people to take responsibility for developing their own skills throughout their working lives. In 1991, the Investors in People Scheme was introduced to encourage employers to link training to business needs and in 1994, recognising

Huw Evans and John Graystone, Chief Executive of Fforwm, answer questions in the House of Commons.

... Pay parity between college lecturers and school teachers in Wales is expected to be achieved within two years, Welsh MPs at Westminster have been told.

But they were also told it will take between five and 14 years before Wales's 25 further education colleges receive the same funding per student as schools ...

that the old apprenticeship models were failing, modern equivalents were introduced, linked to the NVQ system.

In 1994/95, the College became one of the first large institutions in North Wales and certainly the first educational establishment to achieve the *Investors in People* award. A thorough review of human resource practices including staff development, equal opportunities, management and communication led to the prestigious award, subsequently reviewed each year thereafter.

By 1997, the TECs were under political pressure and the newly elected Labour Government abolished them in England, replacing them with broader partnerships called Learning and Skills Councils, which had their roots firmly within the public sector. Also in 1997, the two North Wales TECs merged to form yet another new training body called 'CELTEC'. Training provision contracted by CELTEC focused on a smaller number of robust, flexible, innovative and responsive organisations working across North Wales.

In 1996/97 the level of training income achieved by the College was £600,000, with approximately 250 clients on Training Credit schemes, Modern Apprenticeships and the Training for Work programmes. Despite significant reductions in the level of grant per trainee apprentice with CELTEC, the College contract grew each year as additional trainees were contracted. In 1998/99, the College was successful in becoming a lead bidder, one of only 12 organisations in North Wales.

Mr Glyn Catley, Chair of Governors, and Mr Huw Evans, Principal, *receive the Investors in People award from Mr Bryn Roberts of TARGED and Mr Rod Richards MP.*

New Deal

The 'New Deal' was introduced in 1997 to tackle long-term unemployment as part of the Welfare to Work programme of the new Labour Government. Working through the Employment Service (ES), as opposed to the TECs/Learning & Skills Councils, the programme targeted 18-24 year olds who had been unemployed for six months or more. Following the successful completion of the 'Gateway' phase, which lasted up to six weeks, the Full-time Education and Training option (FTET) was available for one year. Incredibly bureaucratic in nature, but essentially no different from the bureaucracy required for TEC funded students, payment was staged: a start fee, on-programme payments and payment on achievement of qualification.

The College created dedicated staff teams to work with 'New Deal' students and their onerous paperwork, just as it had for TEC funded programmes.

Nancy Dando, Head of Lifelong Learning travels by bus to promote the New Deal initiative.

The Department of Education and Employment

In July 1995, the Department for Education and the employment training and equal opportunities functions of the Department of Employment were brought together under one Department. The aim of the new Department was to increase the nation's competitiveness and quality of life by:

1. Raising the levels of educational achievement and skill for all through initial and lifetime learning;

2. The advancement of understanding and knowledge; and

3. Promoting a flexible and efficient labour market.

In the Competitiveness White Paper 1995, which detailed concerns about the UK position compared with other developed countries, the Government subsequently endorsed a set of revised National Targets for Education and Training (NTETs) which had been extended to include the attainment of core skills and higher level skills. The revised targets were challenging and aimed to provide a clear focus for all those involved in education and training.

The targets for the year 2000 were:

- By the age of 19, 85% of young people would be achieving one of the following: five GCSEs at grade C or above, an Intermediate GNVQ, or a NVQ at level 2.
- 75% of young people would achieve level 2 in the key skills of communication, numeracy and information technology by the age of 19; and 35% would achieve level 3 in these skills by the age of 21.
- By the age of 21, 60% of young people would achieve one of the following: two GCE A levels; an Advanced GNVQ (the equivalent of two Vocational A levels); or an NVQ at level 3.

In addition, targets for the workforce included:

- 60% of the workforce would be qualified to NVQ level 3, Advanced GNVQ or two GCEs at A level standard.

In March 1996, the College set up a work-based NVQ training programme with Quinton Hazell. By April 1997, over 20 employees successfully completed their NVQ level 1 in Engineering Machining.

In March 1996, a full review of qualifications for 16-19 year olds undertaken by Ron Dearing on behalf of the Department, was published. Dearing recommended a national framework of qualifications comprising four levels: Advanced, Intermediate, Foundation and Entry level.

Welsh Office and National Assembly for Wales

Prior to 1999, Wales was governed through the Welsh Office and represented in Westminster by a Secretary of State who was elected without necessarily holding a Welsh constituency. A referendum in 1979 to create a new Welsh Assembly had failed and devolution remained at arm's length until a second referendum in September 1997 approved the creation of the National Assembly for Wales by a majority of just 6,712 votes.

Created by the Government of Wales Act 1998, the first National Assembly for Wales was elected on 6 May 1999. The executive responsibilities were delegated to the First Minister supported by eight ministers, who became collectively known as the Welsh Assembly Government (WAG). Most of the powers of the Welsh Office and Secretary of State for Wales transferred to the Assembly, although initially without powers to initiate primary legislation. Education in Wales, including the FE Sector, became one of the prime responsibilities of the Welsh Assembly Government creating a distinctively Welsh agenda for the evolving FE Sector in Wales.

Running concurrently with these changes was an agenda to deliver prosperity to the people of Wales. In March 1995, a report named *People and Prosperity* was issued. In 1997, *People and Prosperity: Building on Success* was published to show how far Wales had succeeded in achieving inward investment and the National Targets for Education and Training (NTETs).

Immediately after this publication, Peter Hain MP, Education Minister at the Welsh Office, was asked to establish and chair the Education and Training Action Group for Wales (ETAG), which was essentially about more choice for students, improved partnership working and challenging the academic and vocational divide. The Group published its Action Plan in March 1999, which included the abolition of the FEFCW and the setting up of a new Council for Education and Training (CETW) and the abolition of the TECs.

A key objective was to provide a more coherent system of post-16 education based on partnership and collaboration. Community Consortia comprising representatives of all post-16 education and training providers were created to establish coherence of regional provision. This led to the formation of a Community Consortium for Education and Training (CCET) for Central North Wales which comprised Conwy and Denbighshire LEAs, the local secondary schools and local Training Providers. CWLWM, as the CCET became known, was chaired by the Principal and led to greater working partnerships amongst its partners, although it arguably lacked any real permanence as it carried no legislative powers or funding.

Local Governmnent Reorganisation

The Local Government (Wales) Act 1994 was an Act of Parliament which created the current local government structure in Wales of 22 unitary authority areas, either counties or county boroughs, and abolished the previous two-tier structure of counties and districts. It came into effect on 1st April 1996 with the newly constituted Denbighshire County Council and Conwy County Borough Council becoming two of the six unitary authorities in North Wales which replaced the former Clwyd and Gwynedd Authorities.

The Internal Environment

The nineties was a period of very rapid and significant growth and it is difficult to present such an array of change by way of limited narrative. To ensure the time line is presented correctly and to ensure the reader can follow the evolving and speedy ethos of change pervading through the Institution at this time, this section of the book seeks to provide a review of College operations, beginning with the College structure.

From this overview of the College structures and the functional areas, linked closely to the detail of the ambitious accommodation strategy and new curriculum portfolio, we are able to appreciate the rapid growth of the Institution as the new Llandrillo College Learning Network took shape, fulfilling its brief of widening participation and opening up education and training opportunities for all.

Demographic Environment

The economy in North Wales during the nineties was still dominated by the service sector, which provided about 75% of employment in the College's immediate catchment area. The leisure, tourism and hospitality industries provided many job opportunities whilst manufacturing continued to decline. The area was characterised by small and medium-sized enterprises (SMEs) and a high level of self-employment. Unemployment remained generally above the UK and EU average, yet with no real prospects of change, employment opportunities remained static. Out-migration amongst the young continued and increasingly, the College targeted adults as the potential supply of labour within the local economy.

Low wages and a pattern of part-time working supported the College's drive towards modularisation and flexibility, creating systems to accumulate credits for the learning achieved, leading to enhanced prospects of occupational opportunity. Although most organisations operated on small profit margins, over 50% of employers declared their commitment to learning. Training costs and value for money, however, remained critical factors.

College Structure

Whilst it is not the intention to detail every change across each curriculum area, it is important to record the significance of the College restructuring and the progress made across the different areas of the College as they expanded throughout the nineties. Some minor restructuring occurred during the early years but the most significant changes occurred in April 1994 and January 1998. One important change, however, was the appointment of Keith Elliot to the post of Assistant Principal (Academic Planning) following the promotion of Dr Tony Walker to the post of Principal of Deeside College in 1993.

In 1994, the four existing Functional Directorates were expanded to take on the roles of the retiring Vice Principal, Dr Bibby, and the Schools of Study were reduced from thirteen to seven. Within this restructuring, two further decisions were taken: Community Studies was incorporated within the School of Health & Care and the School of Business, Computing & IT was merged with

Science to form the School of Science & Information Technology. To ensure community operations were supported across the region, two Community Co-ordinators were appointed; one in the School of Health, Care & the Community for the Clwyd operations and one in the School of Languages & the Arts for the Gwynedd operations.

1. The School of Languages & the Arts
2. The School of Food & Hospitality Management
3. The School of Leisure & Tourism
4. The Business School
5. The School of Science & Information Technology
6. The Technology School
7. The School of Health, Care & the Community

With the addition of the Learning Support Unit, established to provide educational support for students across all curriculum areas, this created eight operational units. In 1995, Information Technology came under the remit of the Business School and Community operations were reinstated

Keith Elliot, Assistant Principal (Academic Planning).

Jim Bennett replaced Keith
Elliot as Assistant Principal
(Academic Planning) in 1996.

Glyn Jones, Assistant Principal
(Marketing & Clients).

Peter McAlister (right),
promoted to Assistant Principal
(Academic Planning).

as a School of Study. In May 1996, the College created the Directorate of Learner Services & Professional Development as a new operational area, which included the Learning Support Unit, Multimedia and the learning workshops, Professional Development and Media Services increasing the Schools of Study to eight operational areas as follows:

1. The School of Languages & the Arts
2. The School of Food & Hospitality Management
3. The School of Leisure & Tourism
4. The Business School
5. The School of Science, Health & Care
6. The Technology School
7. The Community School
8. Learner Services & Professional Development

By the commencement of the academic year 1996/97, there were two further changes to the management structure: Keith Elliot, Assistant Principal (Academic Planning) was appointed Principal of Swansea College and succeeded in his post by Jim Bennett.

In January 1998, the Principal prepared a very detailed review document on the structure of the College. This focused on the efficiency and effectiveness of the operational areas in an attempt to improve deteriorating financial forecasts and falling student numbers and performance in some areas of the College.

In 1999, Jim Bennett left the College to join HM's Inspectorate and was succeeded by Peter McAllister, the former Head of the School of Languages & the Arts.

These changes, together with the successful promotion of Glyn Jones to the post of Principal of Pembrokeshire College, created an opportunity to make radical alterations to the College's structure.

The Functional Directorates reduced to three to be supported by two Operational Directorates, Corporate Development and Learner Services:

Directorate of Corporate Development (Gwen Parry)	Directorate of Learner Services (Jean Smith)
Publicity and PR	Library & Information Services
External Funding	Learning Support inc. Second Chance
Marketing	Student Services (Advice & Guidance)
Overseas Co-ordination	Learning Network and workshops
Campus Cymru Ltd	Professional and Staff Development (later transferred to the Human Resource Directorate)

The School of Community, no stranger to annual change, ceased to function as a curriculum School of Study, and was restructured and amalgamated with Training Operations under a new operational/curriculum area known as 'Lifelong Learning' reporting directly to the Assistant Principal (Finance & Business Services). The restructuring included many other internal changes, including the creation of a central registry responsible for MIS, admissions and examinations. The restructuring also heralded the beginning of the new Learning Network, with the creation of the new Rhyl College in 1998. During this period every opportunity was taken to review and restructure College operations. Change was necessary to keep pace with the fast moving external environment and the constant drive to improve performance and responsiveness within a corporate ethos. New quality systems were introduced together with new ways of engagement with employers and communities. The College was beginning to establish a national reputation for innovation and responsiveness.

Coinciding with the revised structure was a change in the position of Chair of the Corporation. In September 1998, Mr Glyn Catley retired from his position as chair, whilst remaining a committed and enthusiastic member of the Board. After nine years of loyal service and having seen

Chris Jackson appointed Chair of the College Board in 1998.

the College through the very challenging times of incorporation and beyond, he handed over responsibility to his successor, Mr Chris Jackson.

The Financial Position

As the College entered the nineties, gross expenditure had reached £5 million with income levels set at £2.5 million. By the time it entered the millennium, gross expenditure was over £17 million.

Working within the Scheme of Delegation, the starting point for setting the College budget under the Education Reform Act was the amalgamation of the historical budgets of the four Clwyd colleges plus the centrally held FE Strategy budget. Reduced for the Higher Education allocation

(WAB) and selected 'excepted' items, the remaining balance was then allocated according to weighted student numbers.

Although the calculated outcome was a much enhanced budget for the College, a top-up figure of some £876,000 transitional arrangements, however, required the full effect of the resource change to be phased in over a period of four years. The College budget calculated for 1991/92 was £6,397,000, whereas the budget actually received was £5,670,000. The potential financial gain to the College was at the expense of NEWI, who traditionally had been over-funded – a situation that came as no surprise to the staff of Llandrillo College!

It was this first increase to the College budget that paved the way for the variety of curriculum initiatives planned by the new College Principal and assisted in creating the first College surplus of £100,000 in 1991/92. Despite such a positive start, the situation was short-lived. Relationships with Clwyd County Council began to falter when they imposed severe budget cuts of

Budget statements				
	1989/90	1994/95	1996/97	1999/00
	£	£	£	£
Expenditure	5,195,100	12,371,000	14,542,000	17,291,000
Income	2,489,300	3,635,000	3,409,000	4,330,000
LEA/FEFCW Grant	2,705,800	8,808,000	11,155,000	13,067,000
Surplus	—	72,000	22,000	106,000

£600,000 in 1992/93, which when added to the continuing underfunding meant the College was financially challenged to avoid a major deficit. The timing was unpalatable given that 1992/93 was to become the final year of Clwyd County Council control as a consequence of the forthcoming Further and Higher Education Act 1992.

The 1992/93 deficit was contained to approximately £225,000, despite Clwyd's untimely intervention to downgrade the treatment of ESF grant income and training credit income, to the detriment of the College finances. It is no wonder that relationships soured as the College prepared for Independence, having to carry forward a significant deficit on its income/expenditure account without the satisfaction of ever having received the underfunding due.

The nineties in the years following Incorporation was a time of growing confidence and surpluses. Despite the ungainly entrance with a large deficit in 1993/94, the College was quick to regain control of its finances and begin the process of accumulating reserve balances. With a new student-driven funding model that rewarded the College for its student numbers, the early years under FEFCW control saw a rapid increase in income. By 1994/95, income had risen to over £12 million, rising to £14.5 million in 1996/97 and £17 million in 1999/00. For five successive years, a surplus was added to the College reserves.

The strategy to increase student numbers quickly paid off and the College found, for the first time, adequate income to proceed with the Accommodation Strategy. It is difficult to narrate the speed of change but suffice to say that each year saw a significant number of beneficial changes across all areas of the curriculum. By 1995, the embryonic learning network was evolving.

In 1996/97, the first delegated budget was piloted in the School of Food & Hospitality. By the following year, delegated budgets were introduced across the whole of the College, acting as the main drivers for delivering the strategic vision and the core values of the institution.

The most difficult year financially was 1998/99. Faced with a cut in the unit of funding, a restriction on the levels of growth, a revised actuarial valuation on pension levels which added to the cost of pension charges and a new accounting standard (FRS12), the College was financially challenged to maintain operations yet continue the investment in the new learning network. Efficiency of delivery was paramount, resulting in teaching costs being controlled with vigour to avoid waste and allow new course provision to develop.

The College NetBws, supported by European funding.

As the nineties progressed, institutional and course-based planning became central to operational effectiveness. The Institutional Plan, approved by the Board and delivered by College management, became the yardstick for institutional progress.

European Funding

During the nineties, European funding became an increasingly important area of income within the College. The structural funds programme which ran from 1994 to 1999 consisted of four funds and six objectives. The two funds used by the College included ERDF (primarily capital for economic growth) and ESF (revenue for vocational training), underwritten by objectives 5b (promoting the development of rural Wales) and objective 3 (combating long-term unemployment, helping people excluded from the labour market and promoting equal opportunities).

In the calendar year 1998, the College submitted 26 bids; 16 were approved, one was rejected and the remainder awaited assessment. The sixteen bids totalled £883,000, of which £582,000 related to 1998 and £301,000 to 1999. This compared to £498,000 in 1997.

The fact that many of the bids were submitted on a partnership basis had a significant impact upon the ethos of the developing College and its drive to more inclusive community learning.

Bids which strengthened community links and developed working partnerships locally and nationally included:

- The partnership with TARGED through the Competitiveness funds, funding network links between Rhyl College, Rhyl & Conwy libraries and MK Electrics in St Asaph to promote learning centres.
- The partnership with Denbighshire County Council and ICL to develop the Cyberskills Centres in Llandudno and Denbigh, ultimately leading to the move from Tan y Fron to Denbigh Middle Lane.
- A pan-Wales series of ADAPT bids partnered with the WJEC.
- The partnership with the Digital College in Wales (Coleg Digidol Cymru) to utilise both computer, internet and television technology to extend learning to socially and economically deprived areas, including rural and agricultural communities.
- The introduction of the University for Industry (UFI) programmes.

- E-College Wales – the BA Enterprise. (In partnership with the University of Glamorgan, this was an ambitious project to engender greater freedom and flexibility for the learner, together with a desire to widen participation. Delivered using the Blackboard Virtual Learning Environment, the project paved the way for an increased blended learning approach whilst encouraging greater on-line developments.)

Student Enrolments

As the College entered the nineties, student numbers stood at around 7,500. These swelled during 1990/91, despite increasing competition from other providers and a demographic downturn. The swift extension of the curriculum portfolio to include new developments in Performing Arts, Leisure & Tourism and the Community contributed significantly to the expansion in numbers.

In 1990/91, there were 1,669 full-time students and 7,008 part-time students, a total of 8,677, of whom 58% were aged

21 and over. The full-time equivalent number (FTE) was 2,342, a statistic which was to become the new measurement for the student population. One year later, the total student population had increased to 10,226 (2,722 FTEs) with almost 2,000 full-time students.

After Incorporation in 1993, the College took full advantage of the new FEFCW funding policies of the Demand Led Element (DLE) to substantially increase further education enrolments year on year. This growth continued until 1996/97 when the DLE was removed and its successor, GIF, was removed as quickly as it was introduced. By now the College had topped 14,000 students with some 20,000 enrolments, and although growth slowed, the approach from the helm was to continue to create cost-efficient growth to maintain the strategic development of the Learning Network. By 1996/97, the FTE had risen to 5,183 which included increasing numbers of TEC-funded students and HE-funded students. Of the 20,000 enrolments, 75% were over the age of 19. Enrolment trends had begun to shift towards an increasingly mature and female-orientated profile – the success of increasing flexibility and access through the Learning Network.

In 1998/99, the FEFCW imposed a slowing of growth by reducing the unit of funding and implementing a cap on the growth allowable. This minor 'hiccup' was quickly overcome with the newly emerging sources of income available from European funding, resulting in student enrolments continuing to grow.

By the millennium, with the FEFCW less responsive to student growth, the College directed considerable financial resources into preparing bids under the Objective One programme to support the continuation of the Learning Network and the new student growth necessary for the Denbigh and Abergele Community Colleges. As the College entered the millennium, the total FTE had risen to over 5,700.

The rapid growth in student enrolments is testimony to effective leadership and the ambition of the Institution, whilst reflecting a willingness to adapt and change and develop new modes of delivery within the priority area of lifelong learning. Over 10% of the available population within Conwy and Denbighshire was attracted to relevant and flexible programmes of learning. This was regarded as the highest participation rate in Wales and fully embraced FE and HE provision, community-based courses and the growing popularity of work-based programmes.

Human Resources

Human Resource management was always central to the College mission. As one of the largest employers within the local community and in the knowledge that the greatest single item of expenditure was staffing, the College recognised that its staff were an important and valuable resource. Committed to creating a supportive and stable environment for its workforce, effective recruitment policies, staff development and staff training were seen as vital to ensuring the staff mix was capable of meeting the demands of a constantly changing environment.

This strength of conviction was rewarded in 1995 with the *Investors in People* Award, the standards of which provided the College with the dynamic means to measure effectiveness and review practices as part of continuous improvement. By the mid-nineties, the College had introduced many new-style posts including a work-based assessor, a workshop supervisor and learning resource staff, all of whom were needed to meet the requirements of enhanced student support systems and flexibility.

Following Incorporation, all colleges in Wales faced a challenging time as they negotiated new lecturer contracts away from the rigidity of the old 'silver book' and Burnham calculations. In the summer of 1995, the College reported that it had reached a mutually acceptable resolution leading to the issue of new and more flexible contracts of employment for all academic staff.

Staff appraisal schemes were also extended to all staff. These provided the essential means of identifying individual

Mr Gwyn Morris Edwards, Assistant Principal (Human Resources).

staff development and training needs to cope with the rapidly changing face of education, where information technology was becoming a fundamental part of College life, where the workplace was now extended to employers' premises and where student-centred learning required individual student records. In November 1996, the College won the Beacon Award for the quality of staff development in ILT.

In April 1997, changes to the Teachers Pension Scheme (TPS) meant that educational establishments were required to bear the full cost of pension and lump sums for any member of the TPS taking early retirement. The full cost averaged £70,000 compared to £20,000 pre-1997. This drastically reduced the number of teachers leaving early and led to the near termination of pensionable service enhancement.

At the beginning of the academic year 1989/90, the College had employed some 500 staff, of which 200 (40%) were full-time and 300 were part-time. Support staff represented 21% (108) of the total numbers. By the end of the academic year 1998/99, total staff numbers had increased to over 700, of which 328 (46%) were full-time reflecting the changing patterns in recruitment and the conversion of many part-time contracts to fractional full-time appointments. Support staff numbers had also risen to 230 to meet the increased demands for the stewardship and administration of the increasing portfolio of buildings and the demands for student support linked to increased student numbers at many different venues.

In February 2000, Mrs Ellen Roberts, Principal's secretary, retired after twenty eight years of service. With her beginnings at Barberry Hill in 1957 as a full-time secretarial student, Ellen, like so many other members of staff, can claim her part in the history of Llandrillo College, having worked alongside each of the three Principals who have managed the Institution since 1964.

The Principal's secretary, Mrs Ellen Roberts, retires after 28 years of service.

Accommodation Strategy

Rhos Site

The College buildings had originally been designed to cater for the equivalent of 800 full-time students (FTEs) but by 1990, the student population was over 2,300 FTEs and growing quickly. Remodelling and adaptation had long been a feature within the College but was inadequate to keep pace with expectations and demands. The College recognised that continued and future growth was dependent upon capital funding which was absolutely essential to support the aspirations and quality developments outlined in the new Development Plans.

In the very early years of the nineties, the College was still preparing for tertiary developments and anticipating a new build which would remedy poor teaching accommodation. In 1990/91, with this in mind but recognising the need for additional classrooms and improved quality teaching areas, the College continued the reorganisation of internal space.

The main hall became a learning workshop for English and Maths, the ground floor of the hostel was converted to two classrooms for Art and general use, the travel office was moved to the Sports Centre to create a new teaching space and the electronics workshop moved out to a double mobile. The crèche on 'B' corridor became a five day service and the first HND base room was created on 'A' corridor where the early microelectronics workshop ('chip-shop') had been. By 1992, work was proceeding on new workshop provision and the students from Art & Design were ready to relocate to an area in Llandudno Town Hall.

Llandudno Town Hall.

As the College prepared for Incorporation, Clwyd County Council invested one last time. A new 'design and build' two storey block, adjacent to the hostel – home to Electronics, the Business Admin. Centre, Arts, Community and much more!

The Accommodation Strategy 1993 was designed to deal with the problem of severe congestion on the Rhos campus, appraising the buildings for their suitability within a changing style of education delivery and tackling overcrowding in the classrooms. This also involved removing mobile classrooms and developing a network of outreach centres. It was a building development strategy designed over three phases, each of which was updated annually by way of a new strategy document. It was also an early means of providing evidence to the newly created FEFCW, who would allocate capital funding.

The Hunter report, commissioned by FEFCW, tackled the issue of repair and maintenance and allowed Colleges to use 'Hunter' monies differently to that scheduled, provided the end result

The new Teaching Block.

incorporated the improvement required. On several occasions monies were 'vired' from Hunter to capital projects where build was a much better long-term solution.

Phase 1 of the strategy was essentially about increasing teaching space and, in 1993, the College was successful in bidding for and securing capital monies of £1.3 million from the FEFCW for a new teaching block. This round of total capital funding was the first and last from the FEFCW, as subsequent years required greater levels of match funding through the use of reserves or loans.

Construction on the new teaching block began in August 1994 to provide learning workshop space and general teaching space for Health & Care in readiness for 1995/96. Simultaneously, the College also committed £450,000 of its own resources to provide an extension to the Sports Hall incorporating lounge facilities and a snack bar. The accommodation also provided space for a new specialist Media Studies

The interior of the new students' lounge.

area, all of which represented Phase 1 of the Accommodation Strategy.

Every subsequent year for several years, students and staff witnessed the impact of the Accommodation Strategy. Car parking problems, mud and disruption were commonplace but the list of new buildings was impressive and even the most disgruntled of staff conceded that the Strategy was working. The Planners, however, were not so easily pleased: at every stage of the Strategy, they wielded their stick to ensure the contract included additional car parking spaces which, of course, resulted in increased cost. This was not the only requirement: planning for any further new buildings was subject to the removal of all mobiles by summer 1997 – a double-sided joy in itself!

The new Library & Information Centre, financed from the first major loan of £2 million, represented a complete departure from previous traditional builds. It not only provided a major lending and reference area, it also hosted a network of CD-Roms and access to the Internet. The use of multimedia and open-learning techniques were now integral to the new teaching and learning strategies adopted by the College for the benefit of their students. By the end of 1995/96, the College had 950+ student computers, a statistic envied by the other FE colleges in Wales. In addition, the new Library housed the Professional Development Unit which included staff development and teacher training.

An additional floor was created on top of the old library creating a two storey block to rehouse the hairdressers on the ground floor and the beauty therapy students on the top floor. Additional classrooms were also added above the existing Vehicle Body Repair building, incorporating a a relocation of facilities including the electronics workshop, the 'Purple Palace'.

In 1995, the College announced a 'No Smoking' policy across all campuses. The hostel was never quite the same – the smoke-hazed staff rooms were part of the fabric and to many, a great deal less unsightly than staff and students huddled outside exits in all weathers!

In April 1996, the College presented the Millennium Accommodation Strategy. Using a complex model of 'space norms'

The new hairdressing salon opened by celebrity hairdresser, Trevor Sorbie, who became the honorary patron of the Hair & Beauty suites at Coleg Llandrillo.

College staff meet Sir Christopher Ball who officiated at the opening of the Library & Information Centre.

The Library & Information Centre.

and predicted student numbers over the next five years, space requirements were determined using Space Full-Time Equivalents (SFTEs) to estimate the space requirements for the future. This was then compared to the space available, leaving a shortfall of space that required finance.

In very simple terms, the Millennium Accommodation Strategy envisaged:

- Three main sites at Rhos, Rhyl and Llandudno;
- A separate administrative centre, possibly at Hawarden Road;
- A new outreach centre at Denbigh.

Financing capital projects was seldom straightforward. After the early success of the teaching block and the use of reserves for the Students' Lounge, the College had to become more financially astute as it embarked on securing a portfolio of loans for future building programmes. VAT planning schemes using Fforwm as a facilitator were introduced, relying on the concept of lease and lease-back to spread the burden of the VAT costs across the life of the building. By 1998, the College had

agreed to participate in a pan-Wales lease and lease-back scheme for future new build, also organised by Fforwm, following the introduction of legislation by HM Customs & Exercise preventing the use of the previous lease and lease-back schemes.

Although significant amounts of capital-related funds were provided by FEFCW, the amount was insufficient to meet the needs of the Millennium Accommodation Strategy. To assist development further and maintain the pace of build, the College turned its attention to European/Local Grants. The success of attracting a range of different bids throughout the nineties was a major catalyst in maintaining momentum.

It is perhaps worthy of mention that during the nineties, a successful bid of £800,000 from the European Regional Development Fund (ERDF) was refused. The bid was to create a Performing & Creative Arts Centre in Llandudno, in partnership with Conwy County Borough Council. The original intention to secure two sources of funding for this new build – ERDF and Lottery funding – was never realised as

the larger lottery bid was rejected. The loss of £2.6 million funding demanded a much-reduced specification, which the College considered unsatisfactory. With the imminent expiry of the lease on the Town Hall, the College decided to withdraw and provide a greatly enhanced, purposeful and integrated centre, the Creative & Performing Arts Block, on the Rhos site. The decision meant the ERDF funding was never realised as it was conditional on a Llandudno base.

The official opening of the Creative & Performing Arts Block was carried out by Peter Hain, Secretary of State for Wales. He defined the Centre as a *'tribute to the energy and vision showed by the College leadership'*.

Peter Hain (left-centre), Secretary of State for Wales and Gareth Thomas, MP at the official opening of the new Creative & Performing Arts block.

The major building changes on the Rhos site during the '90s:	Date
The Business Admin. Centre/Electronics workshop – 'J' block	1992
Student Lounge and Media Centre	1994
New Teaching Block	1995
Library & Information Centre; creation of a bus park; widening of College entrance	1996
Higher Education Corridor	1996
New floor and classrooms in the Technology Block	1997
Remodelling of old Library and the creation of Hair & Beauty Centre	1997
Creative & Performing Arts block replacing Llandudno Town Hall	Jan. 1998

The Community Estate

Rhyl Community College.

During the early stages of the capital building programme, the College had begun the process of developing a more formalised Community Network, primarily through leased or rented accommodation. By 1996, the College was facing challenging decisions as short-term leases began to expire on most of the operational bases in Colwyn Bay, Rhyl, Llandudno and Denbigh.

The table below represents some of the many locations utilised by the College throughout the nineties and beyond.

Several sites had already been trialled in Rhyl with an early community venue at Morfa Clwyd in Marsh Road hosting the successful 'Drome' programme. This was replaced with the lease of Building 100 at Cefndy Road following the success in

Formal outreach sites	Date opened	Nature of provision
Colwyn Bay		
Wynnstay Road	1991	College Company
Hawarden Road	1992	Community
Dinerth Road	circa 1997	Community & Administration
Rhyl		
Morfa Clwyd	1991	Drome
Rhyl Library	1991	Second Chance
Cefndy Road – Building 100 and Units 4 & 4A replaced by Community College	1993	Community
Rhyl Community College – old Manweb Buildings	1998	Learning Network

Formal outreach sites	Date opened	Nature of provision
Llandudno		
Town Hall replaced by new build at Rhos	1993	Creative Arts
Education Shop in Victoria Centre – one full year	1993	Advice & Guidance
Cyberskills Centre, Madoc Street	1997	Communication technologies
Cae Bach	1995	Motor vehicle
Denbigh		
Tan y Fron	1991	Community
Middle Lane	1998	Community
St Asaph Business Park		
Elwy Centre	1998	Employer training

acquiring the MSC-funded contract for training students. With the expansion of student numbers and the introduction of IT courses, it became necessary to lease further space on the same site – Units 4 and 4A, most of which was poor quality but adequate in the short term.

In 1994, negotiations had started with TARGED and Rhuddlan Borough Council with a view to acquiring premises in Rhyl. Research revealed a significant demand for provision in the Rhyl area and the College was of the opinion that there was major potential for a successful site development.

In 1997, the College secured the old Manweb buildings in Rhyl on a fifteen year lease. By September 1998, the first major refurbishment had taken place and Rhyl Community College opened its doors, exceeding the 1,000 student target set for the academic session 1998/99.

In 1997, the College in partnership with Denbighshire County Council also secured European funding to host two Cyberskills Centres. One was located at Denbigh

Middle Lane under the management of Denbighshire LEA and the other was located in new College premises in Madoc Street, Llandudno. Derived from a concept evolved by ICL International Computers Limited, the Centres were designed to provide training facilities for small businesses in the use of communication

The building 100 at Cefndy Road (above) and Cefndy Road Open Day (below).

technologies. During the same year, the College began the transfer from Tan y Fron to Denbigh Middle Lane to rationalise provision.

In October 1998, the Governing Body had approved lease arrangements for a new Centre on the St Asaph Business Park to provide dedicated space for commercial training. Conveniently situated above the Welsh Development Agency and in close proximity to CELTEC, it was felt that strategically the Centre represented a nodal point for the future development of employment training in North Wales.

The ELWY Centre on the St Asaph Business Park.

Curriculum Developments

The most significant curriculum developments of the nineties are detailed below. It is however, important to recognise that no one achievement can be viewed in isolation. Indeed, the speed and variety of objective achievement was a consequence of a carefully structured Strategic Plan, incorporating complex financial modelling and allied to a very adventurous estates strategy and expanding curriculum portfolio. Without the buildings and the adaptations, the College would not have achieved the space or quality of environment to meet its increasing student numbers and curriculum aspirations. Each element of the Strategic Plan was placed under constant review to ensure that phasing and optimum delivery was achieved on time and within budget.

By the early nineties, the College should have seen the benefits of a new campus created as part of the Tertiary Plans. This had failed to materialise for two reasons: the removal of the College from local authority control through Incorporation and local opposition from schools who were against losing their sixth forms.

The preparatory work for a tertiary college together with the later plans for Incorporation, however, proved invaluable. They formed the basis for subsequent, successful strategic planning which saw the College position itself as one of the leading UK Institutions, providing a regional, networked, quality and collaborative learning service for further education and vocational higher education, as well as offering personal support for its students and a learning experience of value.

Using the main objective headings set by the new Principal in 1989, curriculum developments are summarised as follows:

Quality – Achievement by Measurement

The College entered the nineties with a commitment to Total Quality Management (TQM). Of significance, and working within the FEFCW Quality Framework, were the appointment of a Quality Manager and the development of the total quality management system initiating the course review system and student/employer surveys. In addition to the enhancement of the staff development budget offering a comprehensive package of training to assist with the many new initiatives, staff residential programmes away from College became an annual opportunity for staff to relax, unwind and share new ideas. With different themes each year, such as 'Implementing New Technologies' in April 1996, the evenings invariably ended in entertainment and fun!

In 1995, a full institutional quality review by FEFCW resulted in all programme areas assessed being above the quality threshold (91% of teaching sessions and 96% of student work ranked from Satisfactory to Outstanding) with Access provision rated simply as Outstanding.

Each year, quality improvements were introduced and student attainment was constantly above the average, with over 94% of A level students achieving Grade A-E in 1998/99. It was in 1998/99 that the College finally secured its place as a leading edge College with one of the highest quality profiles in Wales, which it has sustained to the present time.

With a culture of rigorous self assessment and continuous improvement at the heart of the quality assurance system, the introduction of functional self assessment in 1998/99 added breadth and rigour to the process. This was confirmed by Estyn Inspectors during the external assessments of three areas of the College activities that same year – Educational Effectiveness, Food & Hospitality, and Leisure & Tourism, incorporating Hairdressing & Beauty.

As one of only two Colleges in Wales pioneering Educational Effectiveness Assessment, Estyn commended the College's quality systems, management processes, leadership and governance.

In 1999/2000, the College became the first college in North Wales to achieve the prestigious Charter Mark Award, which rewards Institutions for their quality systems, formal processes and attitude to customer care. The outcome led to a delegation of principals and ministers from Baden-Wurttemberg requesting support from the college in developing their own quality systems.

A contemporary newspaper report praises the College's community approach.

Inspectors commend community outreach approach

College grows to top of the class

A COLLEGE with plans for a big development in Rhyl has been further praised as a flagship for further education in Wales.

Government inspectors have given Llandrillo College the best overall quality profile in Wales after 45 assessors looked at teaching sites in Rhyl, Llandudno and Colwyn Bay.

… The report highlighted its vision in taking Further Education out into the community, with satellite centres which include Llansannan and Rhyl, where a new college for 1,000 students at Cefndy Road is planned for the end of next year.

Student Entitlements

Student support systems were developed as emphasis was placed on a more learner-centred ethos. With the introduction of a Student Services Unit, the College enhanced student support in the areas of guidance, counselling and careers advice.

The growth in student numbers and the increase in adult learners brought new challenges to the Student Support Services. Assistance with financial issues, child care, accommodation, health and personal problems were high on the list of many students and this became a priority development throughout the nineties to ensure student retention rates were not adversely affected.

By 1996/97, Student Support, Admissions and Advice & Guidance were integrated within a new Advice Centre to provide the one-stop shop for enquiries. The same year, formal parents' evenings were introduced to enable parents and guardians to seek direct feedback on how their son/daughter was getting on at College.

Students also benefited from the introduction of a three day induction programme for all full-time students, with an induction module accredited by the Open College Network (OCN).

Open Days had always been a key event in the college calendar year. By 1993, the event had become an all day affair allowing prospective students and their families an opportunity to attend well into the evening. In 1996, the Open Day was on a Saturday, with bouncy castles, ice cream stalls, have-a-go diggers and much more, making the event a family affair.

The College Open Day takes to the road – here exhibiting at the Anglesey Show.

In 1999/2000, the Advice & Guidance team became the first winner of the All Wales prestigious Adult Guidance Award.

In creating a more learner-centred ethos, the College embarked upon a major drive towards modularisation of the curriculum for the purpose of widening access and increasing participation. In 1992/93 some 1,800 modules were written by staff across the College and passed through the quality assurance route to be awarded a credit value by the North Wales Access Consortium (NWAC). In addition, the College played a leading role in the development of the Welsh Credit Framework (CREDIS) to credit rate national qualifications to encourage the take-up of individual modules. In 1996, the College hosted its first commercial national conference, making it a market leader in Credit and Modularisation.

This was supported by the introduction of new flexible learning workshops across three key areas: English & Communication, Maths and IT. Once again the main hall changed in functionality to become the temporary new home for the delivery of English and Maths whilst IT remained in a mobile, also awaiting a more permanent home. The new workshops were eventually introduced in 1997. There was also an expansion of innovative multimedia and related technologies learning materials through the work of the Fairbairn Fellowship, the 'info-net' partnership and the Prospects 2000 programme which included the libraries, five other colleges, Marcher Sound radio and the TEC.

The College wins the All Wales Advice & Guidance award.

A Wide Range of Opportunity

To support the growth in student numbers and increase the range of opportunities, the College introduced new vocational courses across many areas of the College, including General National Vocational Qualifications (GNVQ) in 1992 in an attempt to establish parity of esteem between academic and vocational qualifications.

New systems were also introduced to Accredit Prior Learning (APL), which was of particular benefit to adult learners. Community courses flourished, extending 'bite- sized' opportunities across Central North Wales using the opportunities afforded by European Funding.

New course provision also included the introduction of Performing Arts, new provision in Leisure & Tourism and the introduction of the acclaimed International Baccalaureate (IB) in 1991/92; and, to support Welsh learners, a partnership with Canolfan Iaith Clwyd, later re-named Popeth Cymraeg, was developed to provide Welsh for Adults courses in 1994/95.

Entry and Exit Strategies

The College was eager to ensure that appropriate entry and exit strategies were in place. A college-wide Foundation Programme for school leavers with few qualifications was introduced with carefully planned lines of progression in each Programme Area.

There was an expansion of HE provision across many areas of the College with the first degree programmes in the School of Food & Hospitality Management and Engineering. This included the development of franchised HE courses with HE partners, including the eventual pathway in Business from Foundation level, with no GCSEs, through to a BA (Hons) Business Management and on to a full MBA.

Under-represented Groups

Opportunities for those traditionally excluded from education were quickly introduced, with the extension of Access courses in Humanities, IT and Science, being awarded a Grade 1 during the full institutional quality review in 1995. These programmes contributed significantly to the newly created North Wales Access Consortium (NWAC) which was to lead to the Open College Network (OCN).

In 1991, Access to HE was a new development in Wales which was not universally accepted by Universities. These 'second chance' programmes for adults were pioneered by the College's Access team, led by Assistant Principal Keith Elliot, who had to convince their HE partners that students were not only capable of succeeding at degree level but could be prepared for degree level study in just one year.

In September 1992, a Science Access to HE programme was introduced to the curriculum which became the first validated modular Access to HE programme in Wales. In 1995, the College Access to HE programmes were inspected and awarded a grade 1 – a first for the College.

The modularisation of the curriculum and the introduction of OCN credits supported hundreds of new learners who were able to benefit from a range of accredited programmes on offer throughout the whole of the College catchment area and the network of learning centres across Conwy and Denbighshire.

Prioritising Flexibility

In 1990, the Principal, responding to the need for greater levels of commercialisation, created a College Company, Bay Enterprises (Wales) Ltd. based in Wynnstay Road, Colwyn Bay

Access students celebrate their success.

to manage all commercial activities at a local, national and overseas level. Working across the College, the main intention was to stimulate commercial courses whilst expanding work overseas. The Company focused on three main trading activities: the long-awaited College contract to deliver a 105 place Youth Training Scheme, short courses co-ordinated by the Short Course Unit and consultancy work.

During 1991/92, and for many years to come, the College extended its activities overseas. Working through Bay Enterprises (Wales) Ltd., two management training contracts were developed in Olomouc (east of Prague in Czechoslovakia) – one

with MICOS and one with the Mohelnice Business School. The programmes were validated by the National Examining Board for Supervisory Management, a division of the City & Guilds of London Institute. Using specially written materials by the Business School, 150 students were successfully trained in the first year alone.

In September 1991, utilising the skills of a team of five lecturers on remitted time, and operating from a mobile on the main site, a new unit within Bay Enterprises (Wales) Ltd. known as 'Front Line Associates' was formed. Their role was to begin a more systematic introduction and marketing of an array of commercial courses into

Bay Enterprises (Wales) Ltd secures Russian business contract.

Mr Robert Gleave, Managing Director of Bay Enterprises with Mr Evegeny Brodsky and his Russian party and Mr Huw Evans, Principal of Llandrillo College

Soviet 'coup' brings hope to businesses

A **UNIQUE** link with Soviet industry has been set up this week by a local college — and it could lead to millions of pounds worth of business for this area.

the curriculum portfolio of the Schools of Study. This included a major survey across North Wales to establish employer needs which gave rise to the development of a training scheme for female staff at Hotpoint ultimately leading to a national training award. In January 1995, the company was renamed Llandrillo College Commercial Services Ltd..

By 1998, the company had changed name again, detaching itself more from the College and becoming Campus Cymru Ltd.. The separation however was not beneficial and intervention was soon needed to reintroduce and improve the infrastructure and communication between the two organisations. The changes however coincided with the opening of a new learning centre to meet the needs of employers, with yet another major drive to extend and develop work-based contracts as an integral part of the curriculum. Campus Cymru Ltd. had served its purpose and the College redirected its energies to developing the new Learning Centre on the St Asaph business park as a base for employer related activities.

Responsiveness to Community

From the outset, Huw Evans made it a College priority to develop the Llandrillo College Learning Network to widen participation and develop education and training opportunities for all. This was achieved initially with new outreach centres

An extract from the Weekly News, October 1991, reporting on the establishment of Front Line Associates.

Your chance to invest in the future

Michal Morley (centre) with his team

A GROUP of highly qualified lecturing staff have recently come together to provide a much-needed service for Industry and Commerce.

Based at the Llandrillo College Campus, Front Line Associates is the management division of Bay Enterprises (Wales) Ltd., the commercial arm of the College.

Bay Enterprises has been operating for some 12 months, and during that per-iod it was recognised that a broader, but specialised group was required to meet the challenges of business and commerce.

The Principal, Mr Huw Evans, recognised that need and established Front Line Associates. The unit commenced commercial operation on September 1st, 1991.

Front Line Associates is able to bring together a co-ordinated team of Management Expertise from all areas and disciplines, and provide for industry and commerce a consultancy service and central link or contact point between businesses and the college.

FRONT LINE ASSOCIATES
BAY ENTERPRISES (WALES) LTD.
Llandrillo College Campus, Llandudno Road
Colwyn Bay, Clwyd LL28 4HZ

F. L. A.

in Rhyl, Colwyn Bay and Tan y Fron on the Denbigh Moors and numerous primary schools across North Wales, culminating finally in the new Community Colleges in Rhyl, Denbigh and Abergele. Teams of dedicated community staff were appointed and a range of new programmes including Second Chance, Family Learning and Deaf Studies with a multitude of discrete learning programmes for disadvantaged communities across Conwy and Denbighshire were put in place.

For the first time in its history, the College created a Welsh Language Development Plan which set clear objectives for the achievement of a bilingual curriculum across all areas of the College.

Many of these developments were seen to be ground breaking and led the way for FE colleges in Wales to transform their sphere of activity and their service to students.

Higher Education

Higher Education was expanded dramatically during the nineties. As only one of two FE colleges having direct Higher Education Funding Council (HEFCW) funding for its HE programmes in Food & Hospitality Management and Automobile Engineering, the College embarked on a policy of increasing and improving upon the higher education opportunities on offer locally. This was achieved in two ways: extending franchise arrangements with other HE Institutions to run HE programmes locally and providing appropriate progression links for all vocational areas in-house.

By the end of 1992, in addition to the existing and developing level 3 curriculum, there were four Access routes validated by NWAC and nationally recognized as entry to HE. Some 75% of all Access students took up places on university courses and gained employment.

In 1993, in addition to the more traditional HE programmes being offered, the College developed a fast-track HNC in Business Administration & Business Information Technology in partnership with TARGED. The one year programme designed for the long term unemployed was designed to address the increasing number of students unable to follow the more traditional means of study because of limited finances and personal reasons.

Franchise links became extensive, with Llandrillo College leading the way for FE Institutions in Wales. The FE Teaching Certificate (C & G 730 Stage 3) was validated by the University of Wales, via NEWI. Llandrillo's CASE (Counselling modules) formed part of the MEd degrees at Bangor and Liverpool University.

New franchise agreements were formed with the University of Glamorgan and NEWI with three new part-time HNCs starting in September 1992 – Engineering, Business & Finance and Information Technology. There was no defined pattern of partnership in the early years, the College simply working with those Institutions prepared to offer innovative challenges and increased places. That said, by 1993, the relationship with the University of Glamorgan was gaining in strength as a further two HND

programmes in Business & Finance and Computer-Aided Engineering were approved and franchised, followed one year later with the HND Business Information Technology. This growing relationship was consolidated in 1996/97 when the College became an Associate College of the University of Glamorgan and successfully developed the BA (Hons) in Hospitality Management culminating in an overall income of £500,000.

Although many of the new franchised places were with Glamorgan, the College – at the invitation of the University College of North Wales, Bangor – began work on a University-funded project developing franchise links between the University Sector and the FE sector. The relationship was strengthened by the secondment of the College Access & Franchising Co-ordinator to work on the development of top-up degrees (2+2) to existing HND provision.

In recognition of the growing number of HE students, on Saturday June 25th 1994, the College celebrated the achievements of its higher level students at its first

In the 'College News' in summer 1994, the Principal stated: '... this is a small beginning, but it will grow from year to year, from the forty or so students now, to two or three hundred in a couple of years' time.' By the end of the nineties, the College recruitment of HE students had exceeded 500 FTE and the venue for the graduation ceremony had changed to Venue Cymru.

Mr George Cameron (right), a lifetime sponsor of the College and a sponsor of the learner achievement awards.

graduation ceremony. The proceedings, held at the St George's Hotel in Llandudno, were honoured by the presence of Lord Dafydd Elis Thomas who presented the awards to over 40 successful HND and HNC graduates. There were also awards for outstanding achievements which were made to 15 students selected from across the College.

Strategically, the College estimated that a further 5,100 square metres of space would be needed for HE expansion by the year 2000 for some 1,000 HE students.

The case for separation from FE was powerful and, increasingly, attention was given to a purpose-built HE block, on or off-site. Several options were explored including the old Penrhos School in Colwyn Bay. By 1996, a solution was found; as the beauty students left for their new home, all rooms on 'C' corridor were refurbished and dedicated, in part, to HE studies.

In April 1996, the HEFCW carried out a quality assessment of the Business & Management provision franchised from the University of Glamorgan. The College was awarded the highest possible level of achievement designated as 'provision that is worthy of recognition and reward'. The position was repeated in 1997 with the inspection of Hospitality & Catering.

In 1998/99, the College became part of the UCAS applications and clearing system and was successfully used for clearing in August 1999.

By 1999/00, the College pioneered several new HE developments. As a partner in the Community University of North Wales (CUNW), the College took a lead in developing a number of new programmes including HNCs in Community Development and Environmental Services. In addition, and validated by the University of Glamorgan, the College implemented the first of the new Foundation degrees.

The College's status in providing high quality degree level programmes was also recognised in 1999/00 with the award of further direct funding from HEFCW under the HE in FE inititaive – another opportunity for expansion. This included new HNC/Ds in IT Technicians, Management & Enterprise for SMEs, Fashion Design & Technology and Environmental Planning plus Food Technology with the Welsh College of Horticulture.

Motor Vehicle staff celebrate the success of their HND/HNC students at the first awards ceremony.

ICT Services
(Systems Support)

Although there has been little reference to ICT Services so far, it is without question that many of the developments achieved within the College were the result of a carefully managed and integrated Information Technology Policy. The main challenge faced by the College was to provide a sufficiently robust platform that would provide the flexibility and security for the student record systems and the administrative systems. At each stage of the building programme and with each change in the curriculum and the funding models, the College ensured sufficient funding was set aside each year to meet the challenges of the future.

In August 1992, a College-wide network, using fibre optic cable, was installed and became operational for both students and staff. Staff from the School of Business Computing & Information Technology worked closely with the ACT Services team in designing and implementing a new Admissions database to ensure a planned integration with CMIS and systems for monitoring attendance in the College's flexible workshops. For the fist time in 1992/93, students received identity cards, sponsored by the TSB, Colwyn Bay. The link to the Internet via the Welsh FE Net Project (JANET) and the development of the College website in 1996 simply added to the facilities available for the students. By 1996/97, the College boasted a ratio of 1.5 computers for all FTE students and 1.2 computers for full-time academic staff.

In 1999, the United Kingdom Education and Research Networking Association (UKERNA), now JANET (UK), was commissioned by the Welsh Funding Councils to undertake a detailed study covering the use and potential uses of video-conferencing across the Higher and Further education sectors in Wales. UKERNA recommended the establishment of a Welsh Video Network (WVN) and during 2000, the WVN service was commissioned by the Funding Councils, supported by the European Regional Development Fund (ERDF).

The Principal addressing members of the Community University of North Wales.

Curriculum Operational Areas

Before we leave the nineties, it would be remiss not to provide a quick flavour of developments that occurred within each of the operational areas. For ease of writing, the detail is framed around the organisational structure approved in 1996 concluding with a short overview of the structure as it entered the millennium.

1. The School of Languages & the Arts
2. The School of Food & Hospitality Management

The Annual Fashion Show in Llandudno.

3. The School of Leisure & Tourism
4. The Business School
5. The School of Science, Health & Care
6. The Technology School
7. The Community School
8. Learner Services & Professional Development

1. The School of Languages & the Arts—established in 1991/92, brought together Creative & Performing Arts and Languages & Humanities and remained in place following the 1994 and 1998 restructurings.

School of Creative & Performing Arts—formed as part of the 1990 restructure, linking Hairdressing, Beauty Therapy, Art & Design and Fashion & Textiles with the newly developed area of Performing Arts. Whilst all the areas struggled with severe resource implications, it was Performing Arts that required immediate accommodation support. The situation was resolved with a rented pair of adjoining mobiles hastily erected on the site in August 1990 which allowed Performing Arts to open its doors, on time, to the students of the fully recruited B/TEC National Diploma in September 1990.

As with all areas of creativity, the students were quick to demonstrate their creative skills despite their lack of resources. The Fashion Show hosted annually was always a huge success, as was the very innovative Dinner/Ballet organised at Bodelwyddan Castle. Determined to celebrate their first year of existence with a memorable event, the Performing Arts students worked with the Catering students to stage their concept of a fifteenth century dinner ballet on Friday 10th May 1991, with guests from the Italian Consulate. Using an Italian theme of 'Commedia dell'Arte', in line with curriculum requirements, the students used comedy, dance and music together with a 'horse and cart' loaned specially for the evening performance with a lavish banquet to entertain their guests to a most enjoyable and memorable evening.

The students did not stop; in December 1991 they staged 'Sweeney Todd' in Theatre Colwyn, followed by 'Trans

Commedia dell'Arte event.

Atlantic 92' in May 1992, using the College Refectory and Main Hall as the settings for their Cruise Liner.

Despite the challenges imposed on the area, successes continued. In 1995/96, Fashion & Textiles students won a beacon award for the design and production of premature baby clothes and the NVQ developments in hairdressing were held in high regard across the College.

The brochure advertising Trans Atlantic 92.

School of Languages & Humanities— also formed during the 1990 restructure, had several key aims: to extend and enhance GCSE/A level provision, develop a Humanities Access course, seek to establish the International Baccalaureate (IB) and enhance language provision, including Welsh. By the end of 1991, language courses had been developed for several local businesses e.g. German at Hotpoint, three Welsh courses had been offered to College staff and the Access to Humanities: Literature & Society was secure.

The decision to run the prestigous IB was taken in 1991. Preparations commenced in earnest and following several trips to Hungary and Brussels, Mrs Carolyn Williams, the IB Co-ordinator, enrolled seventeen students on the IB in time for 1992/93, enabling students to combine humanities, arts and science together. As only one of 28 Institutions approved to run the IB in the UK, students travelled from as far away as Stoke-on-Trent and Stockport.

The newly created flexible English workshop was fully operational by

Carolyn Williams, the first IB Co-ordinator.

1992/93, providing for over 150 GCSE students with plans to extend it to include Communication. A flexible learning Language workshop was also created to provide a drop-in service for language learners and summer courses for English as a Foreign Language (EFL) students.

By the end of 1992/93, under the remit of the new School of Languages & the Arts, the College successfully negotiated a lease for space and theatre facilities at Llandudno Town Hall to expand and develop Art & Design. After extensive refurbishment, the College opened its doors to some 200 students in September 1993 in Llandudno.

Although the original intention was to provide new premises in Llandudno, the College finally decided to relocate the students back to the main site. In January 1998, the students returned to Rhos to a new state-of-the-art building, incorporating the very popular Media Studies initiative.

By this time, the School was changing again, incorporating Maths and Science on this occasion in readiness to meet the

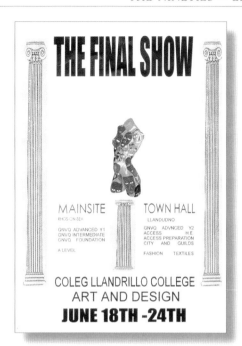

THE FINAL SHOW

MAINSITE   TOWN HALL
RHOS-ON-SEA   LLANDUDNO

GNVQ ADVANCED Y1   GNVQ ADVNCED Y2
GNVQ INTERMEDIATE ACCESS   H.E.
GNVQ FOUNDATION   ACCESS PREPARATION
                   CITY AND GUILDS
A LEVEL
                   FASHION   TEXTILES

COLEG LLANDRILLO COLLEGE
ART AND DESIGN
JUNE 18TH -24TH

challenges of 'Curriculum 2000'. Winning the (DTI) *Languages for Export Award* for the College's work-based foreign language programmes was a significant achievement in 1998/99.

2. The School of Food & Hospitality Management—formerly the School of Hotel, Catering & Food Studies. This area entered the nineties with the possibility of losing the HND programme and the prospect of falling student numbers.

Rising to these challenges, the School soon celebrated a hard-won decision to retain funding for the HND, increased student numbers and began 1991/92 with the opening of new flexible kitchens

Students in Llandudno advertise their final show (left).

and workshop areas, while the staff were trained in the Modularisation project. Already experienced in NVQ programmes, the School extended its provision in Food & Beverage, Bakery and Meat, developing each curriculum within a new modular framework. By 1992, building on the success of retaining the HND and to further

Melanie Monteith collects the DTI Languages for Export award (above).

Three students from the School of Food and Hospitality Management – Jan Sowtus, Bryn Williams and Toby Beavers – selected to represent the College at an international cooking competition held in Maastricht, Holland in 1997.

Students from the Hotel Akademia in the Spis region of Slovakia on an exchange visit to the College in 1996.

boost student numbers, the College opened negotiations to launch a degree programme – the BSc in Hospitality Management.

The School participated in the two major events with the Performing Arts students in 1991 and 1992 and established new European Links with reciprocal staff visits to Inter Ven College in the Netherlands. In 1991, students attended a conference in Paris to look at the implications of 'Hotel & Catering in Europe 1992 and beyond'. European industrial release was also being developed, with students being allocated placements in Belgium, Netherlands, Switzerland and Italy using European

funding under Comett II. Later with the support of Socrates and Leonardo funding, students travelled as far as America.

In 1996, Llandrillo College were asked to provide catering students to work at the Chelsea Flower Show. Twenty three students and 2 kitchen staff found the work hard but rewarding, serving over 200 breakfasts, 400 lunches and 400 teas each day. On the very first day, the students served champagne and canapés to the Queen and the Duke of Edinburgh – a reward in itself!

Although an attempt was made to restructure the area during the nineties to incorporate Leisure & Tourism, the situation was short-lived, leaving the School intact as it entered the millennium.

The School was never a stranger to the newspapers with many student successes. These continued throughout the nineties with a variety of accolades both regionally and nationally. The achievement of the prestigious 'Le Fouet D'Argent' (the Silver Whisk), with the conferring of the title

The prestigious 'Silver Whisk' is awarded to the team from Llandrillo College.

'Best Hotel School in Europe' in 1999 exemplified the international standing of the College's catering programmes.

3. The School of Leisure & Tourism— technically became operational in 1991 with a newly appointed Head of School. A series of retirements and staff relocation steered the way for new course provision, building on the launch of the BTEC First Diploma and National Diploma in Leisure. A noted introduction in 1991/92 was the Certificate of Tourist Information Competence Course (COTICC) run on behalf of the Wales Tourism Board. Working also in partnership with Nant BH Outdoor Education Centre, the School was able to extend the curriculum and develop new outdoor options, adding to rising student enrolments.

Leisure & Tourism staff lend a hand at the Sun Centre, Rhyl.

The Sports Centre served a dual function, providing services for the public in addition to a very comprehensive programme of sports courses and activities for students. During the holidays, the Centre was open for children's activities and in 1996/97, provided a support service for the Saturday morning classes. The fitness suite which opened in 1995 saw a steady rise in the number of users during the remainder of the nineties, but despite continued applications for funding, the all-weather pitch remained conspicuous by its absence.

College sports continued to flourish with teams winning national competitions in hockey, table tennis and football, where both the male and female teams won the All Wales five-a-side football championship. In addition, the sports students gained international success by winning the Russian-British football tournament organised by the British Council.

The curriculum portfolio was in four main areas: Leisure Studies, Travel & Tourism, Hairdressing & Beauty Therapy, the latter two having transferred during the formation of the School of Languages & the Arts. In addition, the School managed the Sports Centre and the College minibuses. In 1990/91, the College Travel Office had relocated to the Sports Centre, providing a learning resource for Travel & Tourism students and a travel service for staff and students alike.

In 1997, the hair and beauty students left their home on 'A' corridor and moved to a new Hair & Beauty suite on the site of the old library. That same year, the College was successful in leading the bid for the All Wales Welcome Host contract under the Wales Tourist Board. In partnership with Bridgend College and Pembrokeshire College, the Welcome Host programmes were introduced to all full-time students as part of their curriculum portfolio.

4. The Business School—During the early nineties, the areas of Business, IT and Secretarial Studies operated as three separate Schools of Study. In the 1994 restructuring, the School of Business Studies and the School of Secretarial and Office Technology were brought together and renamed the Business School, incorporating Computing & Information Technology some eighteen months later when the School of Science & Information Technology was separated.

The early years of the decade are characterised by a substantial increase in full-time and part-time enrolments, dedicated workshops for secretarial and office technology students, a rapidly developing portfolio of Higher Education and the creation of a portfolio of

Staff and retired staff at Llandrillo College claim a double victory over the students in a League 5-a-side Cup competition.

management development courses. The School also began working directly with Bay Enterprises Ltd./ Llandrillo College Commercial Services Ltd., releasing five staff to develop commercial opportunities and overseas training packages.

In September 1992, the first group of Business students enrolled on the Certificate in Management course. Developed to comply with the occupational standards for managers at level 4 under the

A young Darren Millar, elected to the position of Assembly Member for Clwyd West in 2007, getting a head start with his oratorical skills during a business lecture.

Business management students in the Boardroom. Staff will recall the old 'LTC' logo which was built into the wall by the construction students.

Management Charter Initiative, the course enabled practising managers to gain credits towards management NVQs by recognising current competence in the workplace.

Modular NVQs in the administrative and secretarial field were quick to develop, supported by an Administration Bureau – the very first Realistic Working Environment for the NVQ students. Staff were also encouraged to become accredited assessors, a compulsory requirement by the RSA for

assessing NVQs in 1993. The Business Administration Centre was to follow, sponsored for several years by Barclays Bank, providing an office administration resource for the rest of the College.

The BTEC National Diploma in Business which at its peak in 1992/93 recruited almost 100 full-time students, was replaced, along with the BTEC First Diploma, by GNVQs in 1994/95.

In addition to the HE provision being highly commended in the Quality Inspection in 1996, one student was awarded the 'British Steel Strip Product' prize in recognition of her outstanding profile on

the HND Business Information Technology course, exceeding the achievements of any University of Glamorgan students or other franchised partners.

Information Technology courses encountered a boom period during the nineties which saw a rise in full-time and part-time student numbers to over 4,500, an increase of some 185% on the late eighties. This included the newly introduced Saturday provision which typically comprised many computer courses. Following the initial burst of introductory computer courses, these reduced as information technology and communications programmes became

more advanced. The commitment to IT provision was significant in both teaching and 'drop-in' resources with over 1,000 computers on the Rhos site alone.

In 1999/2000, the School of Business went on to win the coveted Beacon Award for developing the transferable employment skills of its full-time students, with particular regard given to innovation and entrepreneurial ideas.

5. The School of Science, Health & Care —was created in 1996 and evolved from a series of changes in the College structure over the first six years. As the College entered the nineties, Science was part of the School of Science, Maths and Electronics. By 1994, it was with Information Technology and in 1996 finally settled in the School of Science, Health & Care. It was also in 1996 that the School of Health & Care lost community provision which once again became the School of Community on its own.

Science had benefited significantly from the refurbishment of 1991, which saw all

In 1993/94, a new training programme was introduced called 'Women mean Business' which gained the College a national training award and the opportunity to expand and develop courses for women returners across the Learning Network.

A celebration of secretarial awards for students of the College.

Students at work in the science laboratories, overlooking the Little Orme.

Nursery nurses (right) get involved in a live project helping a mum with her quadruplets.

In Health & Care, the introduction of the BTEC National Diploma in Social Care boosted numbers, also enabling improved routes to HE. The Children's Act 1991 generated many new enquiries for childcare courses, resulting in a major programme of staff training to meet the requirements of the Act.

The new School benefited significantly from the new teaching block in 1995/96, which provided enhanced facilities for the Health & Care students. Course provision included GCSEs, GNVQs and A levels. In 1996, the area introduced the BTEC First Diploma in Animal Care. Also in 1996, the Duke of Westminster, visited the College to

the Science laboratories, a preparation room and a small resources room located together on 'B' corridor. For students wishing to take science and maths, the College offered these enhanced science laboratories for experimental and investigative work and a Maths Workshop where students could study at their own pace. The Science Access programme for mature students included options in biological sciences, health sciences and environmental science.

meet students following the BTEC National Diploma and Certificate in Land and Countryside Studies.

6. The School of Technology—created in 1994, brought together three previously separate areas: the School of Building & Civil Engineering, the School of Automobile Engineering and the School of Mechanical Production & Electrical Engineering. For inspection purposes, the area comprised two programme areas: Construction and Engineering.

The early nineties was a time of extending open access courses and competence-based assessment. Staff were encouraged to update their skills not only to keep abreast of industrial developments but also to develop greater team teaching to meet the challenges of modularisation. European links were being pursued and for the first time, students enjoyed exchange links with the Dutch Technical Institute whilst working jointly on a manufacturing project.

To support the new School, extensive remodelling of the mechanical engineering

Despite limited resources, the electronics staff found innovative ways of providing programmes of flexible learning for students within the workplace.

workshops began in 1995 to create the new Technology Centre, providing the base for electronics, CAD, electrical engineering and manufacturing.

In May 1997, both Engineering and Construction were assessed using the areas' own self-assessment reports. Piloting the new Quality Assessment Framework for FE in Wales, the College was happy to take the results as part of the longitudinal assessment programme and were pleased at the close fit between internally-assessed grades and those awarded by the Assessment Team. Courses were assessed from Foundation level to the HNC, where work-based assessment and good contact with the industry were seen as a significant feature of provision. The results were a most rewarding Grade 2, although some disappointment was expressed with the grade 2 awarded for the Management of Quality due to a relative lack of peer observation at the time.

Curriculum Area Assessment	
Element 1	
Teaching and Learning	Grade 2
Element 2	
Standards of achievement	Grade 2
Element 3	
Nature and scope of the curriculum	Grade 1
Element 4	
Support for Learning	Grade 1
Element 5	
Management and Use of Resources	Grade 1
Element 6	
Management of Quality	Grade 2

In 1998, 5 electronics lecturers and 8 electrical lecturers took part in a WJEC project on the openness of learning in microelectronics in the newly extended workshop area, with one lecturer on a Fellowship with a remit to look at small companies and education. Later that year, in partnership with Sickens Paints, Motor Vehicle finally got their Paint Spray booth.

7. The School of Community Studies—initiated in September 1991, built on the existing partnerships already formed between the College, local community groups and local education providers, where a large percentage of the delivery was through the medium of Welsh.

The Engineering workshop.

Students work on college cars with 'off-road' personalised number plates.

Acting on the early decision that all adult education classes in North West Clwyd would transfer from the County Council to the College prior to incorporation, the Principal expanded the College community provision using three key outreach centres in Rhyl, Colwyn Bay and Tan y Fron. By the end of 1992/93, over 380 courses were offered in a total of 21 locations.

The consolidation of all adult education provision in the North West proved extremely beneficial, particularly when compared with the provision in North East Clwyd, where the decision by Clwyd County Council to retain adult education, led to a more fragmented development.

Recognition of progression routes was also a key feature of community provision, much of which was validated through the Open College Network. Although the School faced many periods of reorganisation during the nineties, losing

Alun Michael, Welsh Secretary, opens the new Rhyl campus watched by Chris Ruane, MP, Chris Jackson, Chair, Cllr Ann Jones and Huw Evans, College Principal.

status on several occasions, community provision was supported energetically by the College with continued investment and development in new outreach centres.

The Hawarden Road Centre in Colwyn Bay was opened in January 1992, offering a 'drop-in' learning facility with a range of provision including IT, sign language courses, study skills and women's courses. Supported by the Colwyn Bay Friendship Club running Drome courses, students began to gain credits for their modular studies through the Open College credits system.

In September 1993, the Drome programme in Morfa Clwyd in Rhyl ceased and 250 students transferred to new premises in Cefndy Road. The Centre provided the 'Training for Work' programmes and a range of IT courses, Art & Design and Business

Administration. Despite limited facilities, the College continued to expand, taking on an additional unit at Cefndy Road, before moving to the old 'Manweb' buildings and creating the new Rhyl College in 1998.

Tan y Fron on the Denbigh Moors focused on bilingual courses that up-skilled and re-skilled the local adult population. Using the results of a local community audit, the curriculum was expanded in 1992/93 to include teacher training and childcare.

Focusing on the overall strategy for tackling social exclusion, the School targeted disaffected young adults, intergenerational learning initiatives and informal learning programmes. A range of projects incorporating multi-agency and partnership arrangements were successfully implemented including the 'ice breaker' courses, the Tŷ Hafan project for young women at risk in Rhyl, the Rhyl Women's Enterprise Centre providing full-time vocational training for women, the Cornerstone Trust project for drink and drug abusers, the Community Auto's in Rhyl Project (CARS) programme, NETBWS

New college opens

Welsh Secretary Alun Michael unveils the commemorative plaque watched by MP Chris Ruane, Chris Jackson, chair of the college corporation, Cllr Ann Jones and college principal Huw Evans

A NEW era in further education dawned in Rhyl when Llandrillo College's new campus was opened by Welsh Secretary.

The new college on the site of the old Manweb offices is designed as part of a planned process to extend and improve learning opportunities in Central North Wales.

It will increase the number of students passing through Llandrillo College to more than 40,000 in the next five years.

Vale of Clwyd MP Chris Ruane said the new facility would improve the skill base deficiency of the area— regarded by him as of major concern.

He said: "The Rhyl College is the most important development in the economic life of the area in the past generation. It will give the opportunity for the local local people to enhance their skills and enable them to take advantage of the economic opportunities that will arise from the £2 billion worth of European aid that will come to Wales next year."

offering mobile training in the community and the workplace and the Skill Build programmes for disaffected young adults to name but a few, and resulting in the Beacon Award commendation for family learning programmes across all centres.

In 1998, the School changed again and combined with Training Operations to become the new operational area of Lifelong Learning.

Hawarden Road Centre, Colwyn Bay (above).

Students from the Tan y Fron centre.

A national conference on integrating Information Learning Technology (ILT) into libraries and learning resource centres, hosted by the College in 1997.

Will Jones, Head of the Learning Support Unit, with some of his student achievers from the Special Games of 1996.

8. Learning Support and Professional Development

—During the nineties, the College increasingly shifted its emphasis away from teaching to inclusive learning, exploiting the potential of technology-driven learning networks to meet the needs of a wider cross-section of the North Wales population.

In May 1996, a new operational area was created, to focus on developing teaching and learning strategies appropriate for a future curriculum. The Directorate of Learner Services & Professional Development included the Learning Support Unit, multimedia and learning workshops, the Professional Development Unit and Media Services. With the support of the new cross-college Learning & Resources Committee, reporting directly to the Academic Board, enhanced staff development programmes were introduced to extend the notion of credit to support a credit-based and modular curriculum. One of the first new strategies was to address the integration of key skills within all programme areas.

During 1998/99, to ensure that the capabilities of staff matched the requirements of a fast changing curriculum, the Professional Development Unit transferred to the Human Resources Directorate to create a direct linkage between strategic human resource management and staff development.

The College Structure as it entered the Millennium

As the College equipped itself to respond to the challenges of the Millennium, a few further changes became necessary to the College structure.

Corporate Development was restructured when the Director, Gwen Parry, joined the Welsh Assembly Government, providing the opportunity to reduce organisational costs by merging operations within the existing three Functional Directorates. Marketing transferred to the Directorate of Academic Planning and Campus Cymru and External Funding transferred to the Finance & Business Services Directorate. The changes also created an opportunity to develop a co-ordinated overseas

recruitment strategy targeting specific regions to boost student numbers.

One final change occurred within the Schools of Study: Maths and Science were incorporated within the School of Languages & the Arts to become the School of Arts & General Education.

Construction students see in the new milennium.

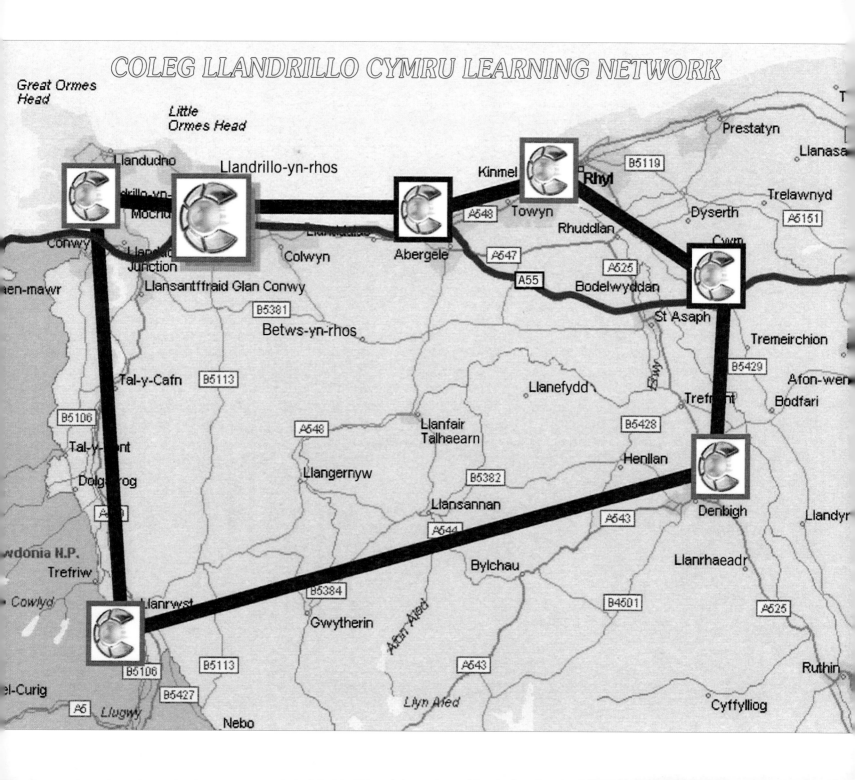

10. Coleg Llandrillo Cymru Learning Network

National Changes of importance

National Council for Education and Training for Wales

On 1 April 2001, as a result of the Learning & Skills Act 2000, the FEFCW was replaced by the National Council for Education & Training for Wales (NCETW), which combined the FEFCW, the four Training & Enterprise Councils in Wales and the Council of Welsh TECs. With a budget of £800 million, it became responsible for the strategic direction, implementation and funding of all post-16 training and education in Wales, with the exception of Higher Education. The publication of 'The Learning Country' in 2001 set out its 10-year plan for post-16 education and training in Wales.

For many, the NCETW was a relatively unknown organisation for it traded under the brand ELWa (Education and Learning Wales). Initially, the ELWa brand was used by both the NCETW and HEFCW, with both organisations sharing a common executive. Following a review in 2002, the Welsh Minister for Education & Lifelong Learning, Jane Davison, decided that each Council should have its own full-time dedicated Chief Executive and Director of Finance and that the two organisations should be formally separated.

In April 2006, the National Council was abolished and its functions transferred to the Welsh Assembly Government, together with the Welsh Development Agency and the Wales Tourist Board to form the Department for Children, Education, Lifelong Learning & Skills (DCELLS).

Estyn

Statutory responsibility for the Quality Inspection of Further Education Colleges and Training organisations also changed on 1st April 2001, passing from FEFCW to Estyn as the office of Her Majesty's Inspectorate for Education & Training in Wales. Funded by the National Assembly for Wales under Section 104 of the Government of Wales Act 1998, Estyn operated as an independent organisation.

Planning for the Llandrillo Learning Network

The Institutional Plans during the millennium reiterated the College's proactive commitment to addressing the issues of social exclusion and increased participation. Such commitment was achieved with the continued development of curriculum initiatives and the creation of a further two Community Colleges in Abergele and Denbigh.

The evolving lifelong learning agenda in Wales with its emphasis on participation and improved access for learners, allied to the space constraints clearly evident on the main site, required a new approach to community learning that was only possible with the furtherance of the Llandrillo Learning Network. The concept of a structured Learning Network, incorporating new campuses and public access points, had become one of the most important strategic drivers for the Institution, despite most of the accommodation strategy up to the millennium being focused on developing the main site at Rhos-on-sea.

To meet the challenges that lay ahead, two new Directorates were introduced at Assistant Principal level. In November 2000, the Services to Business Directorate – incorporating the Virtual Learning Centre (VLC) – was created as a direct response to the needs of business and the local economy. Fundamental to this area was the Director, Kevin Palmer, who, as Entrepreneurial Champion, played a crucial role in the submission of bids from the Knowledge Exploitation Fund (KEF). In April 2001, the Learning Network Directorate was created to further develop widening participation and sustainable community development.

In 2001, residents of the Abergele/Towyn area were invited to sample a few of the courses offered locally by Coleg Llandrillo Cymru during an 'Adult Learning Open Morning' in Towyn. These included computing, art & design, running a small business and many more.

The College launches its new corporate identity and its Welsh development policy at the National Eisteddfod in Denbigh in 2001.

Estyn Grades for External Inspection

In 2002, Estyn completed their five year inspection of the College provision and pronounced the quality profile was 'without doubt the best in Wales'.

In March 2002, Gwyn Morris Edwards retired and was succeeded by Jean Smith as the Assistant Principal (Human Resources) and in August 2002, Gerry Jenson was appointed to the post of Assistant Principal (Learning Networks).

With its refocused management structure, it is perhaps no surprise that the College also decided to review its corporate identity and re-brand to provide a clearer identity for the evolving Learning Network. A new logo, a change in name to **Coleg**

Llandrillo Cymru and a new mission statement were developed alongside a new strap line: 'Learning Excellence in Wales'. The new image was launched at the National Eisteddfod in Denbigh during the summer of 2001 at the same time as the College's newly developed Welsh Language Scheme, which placed a new emphasis on bilingualism and the use of the Welsh language within the College.

By February 2002, however, structures had changed again. Peter McAllister left the College to join ELWa while Jim Bennett returned to his former post of Assistant Principal (Academic Planning). The Services to Business Directorate was restructured into two discrete operational areas – ICT Services, incorporating the VLC and the existing System Support team and the Commercial Support Unit (CSU) reporting directly to the Assistant Principal (Finance & Business Services) who changed title to the Assistant Principal (Business & Central Services). These changes coincided with a realignment of duties across the other Directorates, and the redefinition of the Schools of Study as Curriculum Areas with a Director supported by Heads of Programme.

So the College began the millennium with a changing management structure, the ever apparent drive of the College staff, one of the best quality profiles in Wales and the growing confidence of a maturing Institution ready to tackle the next phase of its ambitious programme.

As we have learned, throughout the entire history of the College, accommodation and funding continued to play a major part in the delivery of the College mission, suitably revised to meet the challenges of the future. The opening of the new millennium was energised by the release of considerable sums of money from the European structural funds, and with so many opportunities to advance the development of the Learning Network, the College quickly prioritised staff and resources to work alongside both County Councils to ensure that college bids represented an important part of the response to the socio-economic needs of the local economy.

Despite the increased pressure this placed on the College, it was a period when opportunities simply could not be missed. The success in attracting major sources of Objective One funding came at a price, however: the first of two planned operational deficits commencing in '01/02. Planned or not, by Christmas 2003, certain ELWa members had become concerned about the Institution's financial stability – a short sighted view, but it took several years of discussion and a very united but steadfast College Board to restore their confidence.

The expenditure on infrastructure, staff and students incurred during the early years of the millennium was really an investment for the future. Set within the national priorities of the day and most firmly within the College vision of an inclusive learning society, the development of the Learning Network was categorised as unparalleled and ground-breaking. With the strength of its management and the unwavering support of its Board, the College demonstrated a level of maturity and confidence that far exceeded those

Jean Smith (above), appointed Assistant Principal (Human Resources) in 2002; and Gerry Jenson (below) became the Assistant Principal (Learning Networks).

Kath Couglin, Assistant Principal (Finance & Central Services), later re-designated Assistant Principal (Corporate Services).

Derwena Watkin, Director of Enterprise

of others in the Further Education sector. To the learners throughout central North Wales, the programme was one of improvement, not upheaval.

In November 2004, Gillian Evans (née Ashworth), Assistant Principal (Business & Central Services) retired and the Directorate was once again restructured. A new Assistant Principal (Finance & Central Services), Kath Coughlin, was appointed and a new Enterprise Directorate was created to include the former CSU under the leadership of Derwena Watkin.

European Structural Funds

By the start of the millennium, the main Structural Funds had reduced from six objectives to three, but most importantly, Conwy and Denbighshire were now included under Objective One which focused on those areas in the EU with low levels of GDP. Coupled with the introduction of the Knowledge Exploitation Fund (KEF), funding was in abundance.

The Welsh Assembly Government had provided funds for KEF to be managed by ELWa and supported by European Union Structural Funds. The purpose of KEF was to provide support for the effective transfer of knowledge, skills and ideas from further and higher education institutions to industry, in order to stimulate the knowledge economy of Wales by way of entrepreneurship and innovation. In terms of both revenue and capital, this source of funding provided much-needed monies to bring FE colleges, in particular, into the 21st century.

The KEF was a real bonus; it did not require match funding by the College. In line with the Structural Funds, KEF Phase 1 started in 2000 and finished in 2002 and was replaced with Phase 2 which began in 2003 and finished in 2006.

Network Responsiveness and European Funding

The millennium therefore was a time when Objective One funding enabled the College to contribute to local and regional regeneration through the provision of training opportunities and learning centres, utilising valuable staff management expertise gained in tackling social exclusion and widening participation. In line with the Millennium Accommodation Strategy, the Business & Central Services Directorate was tasked with co-ordinating all College bids to ensure that European monies were secured to support the new Community Colleges, introduce new curriculum ideas, sustain the rate of growth and keep pace with research, innovation and development using earmarked College reserves.

Securing funding for much-needed capital was only one consideration. The College desperately needed revenue related bids to provide the growth for community-driven and training-led learning. Despite the promise of a funding review by ELWa to support widening participation, this did not happen in the early years of the millennium, so the two new Community Colleges used short-term ESF funding and 'borrowed' funding units from the rest of the College until their new growth was secured and consolidated or funding realigned internally. Although revenue support from the capital grants supported key personnel in the first years of development, the Community Colleges were, like other curriculum areas, immediately under pressure to develop a sustainable and consolidated curriculum to guarantee financial viability after three years of operation.

The Assistant Principal (Learning Networks) was never short of a challenge; with a series of five major revenue bids affecting the community budgets in the first part of the millennium, maintaining part-time lecturer spend was probably the biggest challenge of all. With the opportunities arising from the Structural Funds programme scheduled to end in 2006, the College clearly felt under some obligation to exploit whatever funding came its way. This was a particularly challenging period in the life of the College but, equally, it must also be heralded as a particularly rewarding one.

It must also be recorded that like its predecessor, the new Millennium Accommodation Strategy was equally ambitious with many evolving curriculum plans running concurrently with building developments. Like all College strategic plans, ambition was matched by flexibility and the ability to respond quickly to unplanned circumstances.

Creation of the Learning Network

The introduction of the embryo Rhyl College in 1998 and the Millennium Accommodation Strategy resulted in a planned approach to creating the Learning Network. The successful launch of Denbigh Community College in August 2001 and Abergele Community College in 2002, both funded via the European structural funds, provided the development hubs for the extension of the Learning Network.

Built around partnerships with a Local Authority and a secondary school, these strategically placed centres in Denbigh and Abergele contributed to the tackling of under-achievement and the development of local economies to help build Wales as a 'learning' country. They were seen as collaborative ventures, ahead of their time.

The growth arising from these Community Colleges, with renewed partnership with local libraries, reflects a degree of generic provision with identified specialisms and responsiveness to local need. This

Denbigh Community College, opened by Rhodri Morgan, First Minister of the National Assembly for Wales in August 2001, was built on the site of the town's 19th century butter & cheese market, which later became a brewery (below, left). The new college incorporates the ground floor and entrance of the older building.

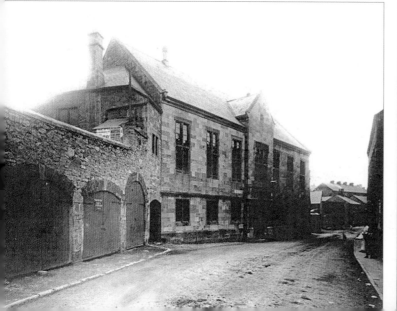

included vocational provision, ICT training, University for Industry (UFI) programmes and on-line developments, as well as provision targeted at improving participation and progression such as Basic Skills, Access to FE etc.. Links with secondary schools in Denbigh for twilight AS subjects were encouraged, as was a dedicated twilight programme at Abergele for post-16 learners from Ysgol Emrys Ap Iwan, the College's partner in the Abergele development.

The creation of Denbigh Community College was the first tangible practical outcome of Objective One funding in Wales, creating a major community resource to assist in reviving the socio-economic needs of the region. Using a combination of ERDF grant and FEFCW/ELWa capital allocation to finance ICT/Equipment infrastructure, the building was secured by way of a long-term lease.

One year later in 2002, Abergele Community College was created using a particularly complex mix of funding streams. The first phase of development began in September 2000 with help initially by way of a National Opportunities Fund (NOF) revenue bid. This was then supported by an ERDF grant, together with ELWa and Conwy County Borough Council support for capital to meet ICT/Equipment infrastructure. With Ysgol Emrys Ap Iwan providing the land and building, Coleg Llandrillo provided the match funding to carry out the remodelling works.

The success of the ESF revenue bids to support the early developments of the Learning Network was critical for the growth of these new Community Colleges.

Alun Pugh, Deputy Education Minister and Assembly Member for Clwyd West, a former College Head of the School of Business & Professional Studies, declares the Abergele Community College open in 2002.

Not only were these bids ground-breaking and highly innovative, but they provided the much-needed finance to support the futures of the Community Colleges. They included:

- The earlier Family Learning programmes followed by Community Enterprise programmes. The Community Enterprise project successfully targeted people from socially and economically deprived areas with few or no qualifications, no work experience and limited access to the labour market back into education.

- The Peripatetic Outreach Programme (POP) 1 and 2. The POP project was led by CHWEAN and involved colleges across North Wales as well as Careers Wales. The recruitment of outreach workers in Denbigh and Llanrwst assisted in engaging with new target groups.

- The People's Network of Learning provided extended ICT links to libraries to assist in the teaching of essential skills. The official launch was held at Rhyl Library and was attended by the Minister, Jane Davidson, and ELWa Chair, Sheila Drury.

- Aspire and Access to FE in the Community effectively built on the success of the other ESF projects, encouraging participants to continue their education in the Community Colleges.

- The Rhyl Women's Enterprise (1 and 2) offering four pathways for women in Plumbing, Gardening, Painting & Decorating and Motor Vehicle. The 'woman centred' ethos of the project enabled many women to gain confidence and overcome personal issues. The unique role of the advocate was invaluable in providing support for students.

- The Vocational Futures Programme which was a partnership bid with the LEAs, Career Wales and the schools to support disadvantaged pupils gain NVQs.

Huw Evans, Principal, Betty Williams, MP, and Irene Norman, Head of Rhyl Community College, at the Beacon Award Ceremony in London in May 2002.

In 2002/03, the College was rewarded for its efforts: a prestigious award from Fforwm for increasing and widening participation in Further Education.

The Technology Directorate

Working also within the National Economic Development Strategy (NEDS) agenda and to continue the process of remodelling the curriculum to meet the needs of the 21st Century, the College accelerated the process of change by prioritising developments from within the Technology School.

In 2001, all colleges in North Wales were asked to submit their Engineering Strategy to ELWa (North Wales Region). Limited capital investment over many years had restricted the growth potential of training in engineering, and rapid technological advances within the motor industry meant SMEs faced stiff competition and were vulnerable to job losses or closures. Using one of the most competitive processes seen by the College, ELWa considered each strategy and allocated funds

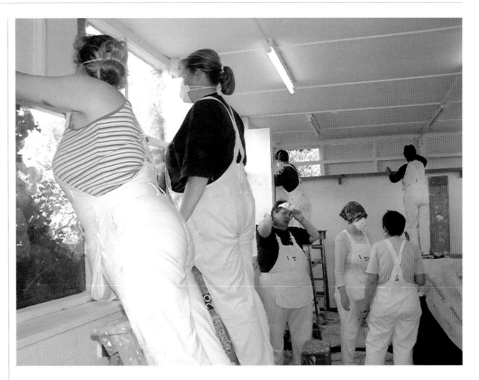

accordingly – funds that were free of any European financial support.

At Coleg Llandrillo Cymru, investment in Motor Vehicle was seen as the first stage of the strategy. The footprint was for a new purpose-built Motor Vehicle Centre adjacent to Rhyl Community College, using the existing building infrastructure of a depot formerly used by Manweb vehicles. This move was intended to facilitate the

Students on the Women's Enterprise programme studied Painting & Decorating as one option of the overall programme which included motor vehicle repair, computer servicing, gardening and more.

release of space on the Rhos-on-sea campus and create the second phase: a new Engineering Centre, a Building Skills Centre and, longer-term, the development of Marine Engineering.

Initially there was some disappointment as ELWa did not support the total investment required, but with the added success in attracting KEF funding, additional monies were eventually secured to complete the first and major components of the Engineering Strategy.

Using Phase 1 KEF capital monies to support technology transfer and £300,000 of the College's own money, the College began the process of relocation, focusing on the provision of new facilities and a new curriculum in Motor Vehicle to meet the standards required by the industry. In April 2003, the Centre for Automotive Technology (CAT) was complete, with a main Motor Vehicle workshop, vehicle body repair area, a spray booth, classrooms, staff rooms, specialist Motor Vehicle operational facilities and a physical link with the existing Rhyl College.

By April 2003, the new Centre for Automotive Technology was complete creating a spacious workshop capable of hosting exbibitions for the motor trade.

Initially, the intention to relocate Motor Vehicle to Rhyl was not universally welcomed by all staff. However, when the scale and scope of the new facilities became evident, even the most sceptical agreed that the move heralded not only the possibilities for Motor Vehicle development but also marked the beginning of a new era where the influence of Coleg Llandrillo Cymru could now be identified with locations other than Rhos-on-sea.

With the buildings in place, the College then secured KEF Phase 2 funding to develop a Centre of Excellence through a technology transfer bid to provide both a physical and a Virtual Learning Environment, where computer technology was used to create and enhance flexible learning opportunities to deliver a comprehensive range of qualifications and practical job-related learning. The opportunities provided by the release of space on the Rhos Campus allowed for the second phase of major development: to redevelop the Engineering Centre. Having attracted £544,025 of ELWa capital (European-free) funding, this was matched against an ERDF bid to meet the total cost of refurbishment. The new Technology & Innovation Centre included a major upgrade to the workshops and facilities, rapid prototyping and an advanced robotic manufacturing cell.

The Technology & Innovation Centre (exterior and interior, below) placed the College in a pivotal position to support engineering in North Wales providing a first class learning environment.

Although the Building Skills Centre was not a beneficiary of the capital European monies outlined above, it did benefit from the release of space which was adapted to provide a much-needed area for plastering, artexing and tiling to support the rapid growth in the local construction industry.

To complete the programme within the Technology School, the College also established a new Gas Training Centre in rented premises near to the Rhyl College in partnership with the Gas and Water National Training Organisations (GWINTO). After a short programme of bespoke structural adaptations, the College was rewarded with the first and successive intake of students all completing their programmes successfully and securing jobs.

Directorate of Hospitality

In 2001/02 the College was awarded Network of Excellence Status for Catering & Hospitality by ELWa, reflecting its national and international reputation.

First Minister for Wales, Rhodri Morgan, at the opening of the Heartspace which transformed the frontage of the College.

BUCKINGHAM PALACE.

I am delighted to have this opportunity to offer my congratulations and best wishes to the past and present Governors, Staff and Students on the great success of Coleg Llandrillo since I had the pleasure of opening it in 1965.

Size is not necessarily a measure of quality, but the College has good reason to feel proud of the further and higher education service it provides for the people of North Wales. The opportunities offered by the College for basic skills training, Modern Apprenticeships, NVQs, A-levels, HNCs, HNDs, Foundation Degrees and Post Graduate Studies are vitally important in helping people to develop their talents and to find useful employment.

I am pleased to know that its efforts have been rewarded by a number of prestigious awards. I have no doubt that the College will become even more successful in the years ahead

Working closely with Centres of Vocational Excellence (COVEs) in England, the College gained recognition for its work with the World Skill Olympics, advising Ystrad Mynach on the redesign of its Hospitality Department and providing culinary demonstrations at the very first Gwledd Conwy Feast in October 2005.

To assist the College with upgrading its facilities, the College was awarded a Technology Transfer project under KEF, which included developments to the Hospitality building infrastructure. The resulting state-of-the art kitchen facilities, with glass walls to allow the diner to see the food being prepared, not only enhanced teaching and restaurant facilities but was an integral part of the long-awaited 'Heartspace' project which was completed in 2003 using the College's own funding.

Heartspace

The 'Heartspace', costing £3 million, was part of the original Estates Strategy. This was the showpiece: the transformation of the old College frontage and reception to a new vibrant entrance, complete with welcoming facilities fit for the millennium. It was finally completed in September 2003 and transformed the entrance to include a new foyer, breath-taking stairway, restaurants, student welfare areas, a travel shop and a conference centre. The building was heralded a major success by the student body, the Hospitality Industry and above all, the College staff. Student Guidance and Support systems were enhanced considerably providing a front-

The Network of Excellence in Hospitality & Catering provided an opportunity for greater partnership and collaboration to improve the availability and quality of training.

Dr Shyam Patiar, Director of Skills Development, formerly Head of Food and Hospitality.

A night to remember. Flash flooding during the College Open Evening in 2001 caused extensive damage to College buildings.

Brian Swindells (left), the College Estates Manager takes the opportunity to show former County Project Architect, Mr Ron Jones the array of changes made to the Rhos Campus since his original designs for the new College way back in 1964.

of-house service for students requiring information, advice and support.

The design was also well received by the former project architect, Mr Ron Jones, who was responsible for the original College design back in 1964. In 2010, he joined the Estates Manager, Mr Brian Swindells, on a tour of the College talking over old times and old designs.

After such an impressive list of programmed building works, it would be remiss not to mention the one major building programme that was not planned and cost the College insurers £500,000, following freak weather conditions during the College Open Evening in July 2001. A deluge of rain led to rainwater cascading off the recently resurfaced coach park, down the steps opposite the hostel, along 'A' corridor and down the link corridor to the old hall, causing extensive damage to buildings and equipment.

Despite the seriousness of the situation that evening, there are many memorable incidents which are remembered with

humour by the College staff who battled to halt the advancing waters and clear the College of prospective students. To the old lady who roamed the corridors and refused to go home, we wish you had taken a mop; to the caretaker who climbed the roof to clear away a seagull's nest and divert water away from the IT server room, we offer you our thanks; and for those of you who found your biscuits missing in the morning, blame the staff who stayed till midnight cleaning up the mess and the Refectory Manager who diligently locked all his food cupboards before the rains came.

ICT Infrastructure

Significant change in the ICT infrastructure also became necessary to extend and develop on-line communication and learning from the Community Colleges, the ELWY Centre and other remote locations. Following the merger of the VLC and the Systems Support Team, ICT Services under the leadership of Aidan Sheil became responsible for the College's technical infrastructure and the development of IT-based teaching and learning materials. They began the millennium with considerable pride by ensuring the notorious 'millennium bug' never made its entrance.

By 2002, the College had some 1,200 computer terminals, all with internet access. Replacement and maintenance of the Learning Network had to be systematic to ensure all learners had access to up-to-date computer technology. In 2002/03, the College required £150,000 to replace and maintain the Network plus £75,000 to upgrade the student records system, improve personnel recording to meet the demands of Estyn and introduce a new enquiry system to aid enrolment.

Committed to the introduction of a fully credit-based and modular curriculum, the millennium witnessed the drive to extend resource-based learning and the new technologies. The e-learning agenda demanded a very new approach to teaching and student engagement, and it is clear that the College, whilst committing significant resources to the challenge, worked closely with other colleges and providers to develop appropriate learning materials and sustain lecturer involvement.

The newly created ICT Services was influential in maintaining the momentum, developing systems that could support both the administrative demands of the curriculum and the demands of the curriculum itself. The IS/IT Committee was established as an Advisory Body to recommend expenditure priorities to ensure resources were used to maximum effect. The demands were great: they included the need to provide a uniform infrastructure across the Network, Internet access for all, web-based learning programmes and a Managed Learning Environment (MLE) to support student tracking systems.

Adopting Moodle as the College Virtual Learning Environment (VLE), students

Aiden Sheil, Director of ICT Services, responsible for the College's technical infrastructure and the development of IT-based teaching and learning materials.

Louise Jowett, Director of Student Recruitment.

A group of international students pose for the camera with Louise Jowett, Director of Student Recruitment.

enjoyed off-site and out-of-hours access to learning materials and communication. The adoption of Moodle and the decision to place emphasis on the European Computer Driving Licence (ECDL) and units from Learn Direct were key factors in developing an e-learning curriculum fit for the 21st century.

Client Demand

Back in 1989, Huw Evans had declared that developing a student focused approach to learning was a key component for a successful college. As we enter the millennium, it is clear that this continued to be a very high priority; whether it was learners in the College, the community, the workplace or simply those using virtual technology. In February 2003, the Principal, Huw Evans was rewarded for his work with an OBE for services to Further Education.

As part of the strategic planning processes, the College continued to review the curriculum offer to meet the initial and progression needs of a widening range of students. By extending opportunities and choice and ensuring a healthy mix of academic and vocational qualifications, the College worked with students to provide personal guidance and support with an integral learning programme as required.

In September 2000, the College successfully implemented 'Curriculum 2000' which was the reform of the A level examinations in the United Kindom designed to give sixth-formers a broader range of subjects with the creation of new AS levels. By incorporating the new vocational A levels (AVCE) with the new AS levels, the College designed a curriculum to widen choice and break down vocational and academic barriers.

All full-time students were also required to undertake the Key Skills award to enhance their programmes of learning and all substantial part-time students undertook some Key Skills relevant to their area of study. Key Skills and Basic Skills Champions were appointed across the Network to ensure Key Skills were integrated into the curriculum, providing the appropriate staff support as necessary. In 2003/04, eleven Bilingual Champions were also appointed across the Network, tasked with encouraging and developing a bilingual curriculum across the Programme Areas.

As A level pass rates continued to rise, the College received the acclaim it wanted: to be one of the national pilot centres for the new Welsh Baccalaureate. In 2003/04, to provide a more integrated experience for learners aspiring to study at level 3 and beyond, the Centre for Advanced Studies was refurbished to provide dedicated facilities and resources for all students studying AS/A levels, the IB and the Welsh Baccalaureate. Developed to provide a focal point for the younger learners on these programmes, the Centre was considered an important component in improving progression and preparing students for the future demands of higher education.

On a less positive note, in 2003, Fashion & Textiles was withdrawn from the curriculum as a consequence of the decline in local manufacturing industry and falling student numbers.

International recruitment also started to grow with students from a number of countries including China, Japan, India and the Middle East. Working closely with agents abroad, College advisors offered a comprehensive English Language provision to support students at all stages within their A level programmes, HND programmes or even pre-master's level. In 2004, the Marketing Department and the International Unit combined to become the Directorate of External Affairs.

By 2004/05, 21,000 students attended College sites with thousands of new learners recruited as a direct consequence of the new Learning Network.

Maggie Griffiths, Director of Health, Wellbeing & ILS.

Responding to the Workplace

The Commercial Support Unit (CSU), supported in part through KEF/Objective One funding, became the new operational area responsible for the training contracts, external contracts with other providers and two large European employer-related bids in partnership with ELWa and other colleges. Based at the relocated ELWY Centre on the St Asaph Business Park, directly above the former CELTEC offices, and with an initial budget of £1,600,000, the CSU became an important steer for developing links with employers, including the first Foundation degree programme with DARA and North Wales Training and on-line training programmes including Health & Safety. Such was the importance of the Foundation degree programme that a member of the College HE team was seconded to work with the CSU.

At the forefront of change, the new bids provided resources for a new type of staff contract – the Business Development Adviser. These were neither teaching nor technician posts. Their roles focused on assessment in the workplace and demanded considerably more flexibility than many other posts, working at weekends and evenings when required. Administration skills and a very personal type of management were also required to monitor and record the complex and rapid turnover of students who ranged from short courses to long-term NVQs.

Another key component of the CSU was its role in national contracts working with the support of third parties. For example, in partnership with Hays Skills Development and Mainport, the College targeted employees in the telecommunications sector to undertake NVQs in Call Handling. The management of these contracts, through detailed memoranda of agreement, was extremely complex both in terms of finance, monitoring and student recording but extremely valuable in raising the number of funding units. During the early part of the millennium, growth was rapid with CSU staff travelling regularly to Birmingham, Cardiff and beyond.

Outstanding Quality

'It is rare that one event lights up a whole year like a beacon – especially when that one event lasts for two fairly harrowing weeks and is preceded by years of hard work ...'

Chris Jackson OBE (Chair)
Annual Report 2004/05

Selecting the areas of significance for the College during the second half of the decade has been extremely difficult. At no point has this powerful institution wavered: there may have been delays, setbacks or even substitutions but fundamentally the strategic vision and leadership has remained and continued to position the College at the leading edge of teaching and learning within the FE sector.

As the College continued through the new millennium, one event was to dominate and characterise college progress: the Institutional Inspection of 2005. That event, under the careful management of Jim Bennett, the Assistant Principal (Planning & Standards) placed the College

as the very best in Wales. The evidence below speaks for itself:

'At present this is the most successful profile of inspection grades for FE colleges in Wales.' (Estyn 2005)

The Inspection team judged the college's work as follows:	Grade
1. How well do learners achieve?	1
2. How effective are teaching, training and assessment?	1
3. How well do the learning experiences meet the needs and interests of learners and the wider community?	1
4. How well are learners cared for, guided and supported?	1
5. How effective are leadership and strategic management?	1
6. How well do leaders and managers evaluate and improve quality and standards?	1
7. How efficient are leaders and managers in using resources?	1

With confirmation from Estyn that Coleg Llandrillo Cymru had the most successful profile in Wales, it is fitting to see the success of the quality systems confirmed over and over again during these final years of the historical record of the College.

Jackie Doodson is appointed Assistant Principal (Academic Planning) upon the successful promotion of Jim Bennett to the post of Principal of South Tyneside College.

Chris Smith, Director of Technology & Innovation.

Following the success of the 2005 inspection, the Principal titled his input to the College's annual planning conference as 'Good to Great' drawing on the work of the management guru, Jim Collins. Leading edge performance and continuous improvement was to become an underpinning requirement for the coming years and the results and outcomes detailed below clearly support this direction of travel.

In total, four further Quality Inspections demonstrated the same level of success over and over again, reinforced by a national award for quality:

- The Adult Community Inspections in Conwy and Denbighshire in 2005 and 2006, working with partners across the counties of Conwy and Denbighshire, were rated excellent.
- Reassessment for the Charter Mark in 2006 scoring 62 full compliances out of a possible 63. By 2007, all 63 criteria had been met.
- The Work Based Inspection in 2008 scored straight grade ones, the highest grade possible.

- The Quality Assurance Agency review of HE programmes in 2008 reported that the College managed its provision extremely well which was an excellent achievement for an FE College.
- The Fforwm Award for 'Leading Innovation in the Management of Quality' in 2009.

The Final Stage of our Journey

The final half of the decade saw yet another change at national level. ELWa was abolished and in April 2006, DCELLS was created to improve children's services, education and training provision in Wales with a view to securing better outcomes for learners, businesses and employers, as set out in the Welsh Assembly Government's strategic document *The Learning Country and its agenda for action – Vision into Action*.

The College entered this final period with a generally strengthened financial position. After years of investment and the run down of College reserves, 2005/06 was a year of consolidation and a return to a healthy surplus. With an equally ambitious

Estates Strategy planned from 2006, financial surpluses were once again an important part of the strategy.

Throughout the remainder of the decade, with strict budgetary controls in place, the College can be justifiably proud in reporting surpluses in excess of £1.3 million each year. This provided the financial headroom to continue the modernisation of the College estate and to provide the resources to match-fund grant aid from the College financial reserves.

Before we present our final chapter, it is fitting at this point to set out the College Structure once again, a structure that reflects the post holders in place prior to the merger in 2010. The Senior Management Team of the College included the Principal and the four Assistant Principals supported by nine Directors of the Curriculum & Functional Areas. Each Director is in turn supported by Heads of Programme of key curriculum and functional areas.

COLLEGE STRUCTURE CHART

**FUNCTIONAL AREAS
—ASSISTANT PRINCIPALS—**

Corporate Services
Kath Coughlin
Personnel Services
Jean Smith (Deputy Principal)
Planning & Standards
Jackie Doodson
Participation & Development
Gerry Jenson

**DIRECTORS OF CURRICULUM
& FUNCTIONAL AREAS**

ICT Services
Aidan Sheil
Student Recruitment
Louise Jowett
**Arts, General Education
& Education & Training**
Kay Wilkins
Hospitality, Business & Tourism
Kevin Potts
Enterprise
Derwena Watkins
Health, Wellbeing & ILS
Maggie Griffiths
Technology & Innovation
Chris Smith
Coleg Llandrillo Rhyl
Celia Jones
Skills Development
Shyam Patiar

Kevin Potts, Director of Hospitality, Business and Tourism.

Kay Wilkins, Director of Arts, General Education and Education & Training.

Two retirements which affected the College Board of Governors should also be noted:

In May 2005, Councillor George Johnson, MBE, announced his retirement from the Board, with effect from the end of the academic year. A long-standing College Governor, the Board placed on record their thanks for his outstanding contribution to the work of the Corporation Board over many years.

Mr George Johnson (above), long-standing College Governor; and Mr John Bellis (below), new Chair of Coleg Llandrillo Cymru.

In the summer of 2006, Chris Jackson stood down as Chair and resumed his place as a Board member. After eight years of dedicated service, Chris recorded in his final Annual Report as Chair, his '… *good fortune to have been associated with the College during a period of unprecedented progress*'. His successor, John Bellis, was an established Board member who brought to the position his experience as a senior executive from the private sector and his local standing in the Rhyl community.

Strategic Priorities

Underpinning the continuing success of the institution was a constant process of review, which saw the later years of this decade focused on the regional economy with targeted support for local community regeneration. Working in partnership with schools, county councils, employers and the emerging Sector Skills Councils (SSCs), a range of strategic priorities encompassing the Learning Network were redefined and re-emphasised to reflect new initiatives and challenges as the College moved into each successive year.

This coincided with the introduction of the new National Planning and Funding System (NPFS) which did little to support the part-time learner and clearly favoured the recruitment of full-time 16-19 year olds. In the light of the above, the Principal made a very deliberate and important decision: to increase full-time numbers whilst continuing to provide education and training opportunities beyond the funded targets, within the parameters of the overall College budget.

The strategic priorities outlined below responded to Welsh Assembly Government National Policy imperatives, the Regional Statement of Needs and Priorities and the Annual Recommendations for Learning supported by the Community Consortia (CCETs) for Conwy and Denbighshire. The key priorities, during the period 2006-2010 included:

Improving the Quality of Education Provision

As part of the process of self-assessment, the College built on the rigour already introduced by the internal inspections and peer appraisal systems, embedding new technologies and the systematic monitoring of outcomes.

There was an increase in bilingualism and Welsh medium delivery which saw the creation of the Bilingual Unit with clear targets for Welsh medium assessment, bilingual delivery and new Welsh medium programmes. Using the Common Investment Funding (CIF), the College partnered with local Welsh medium schools to provide progression opportunities for Welsh speaking students. By 2007/08, the numbers of learners had increased by 11% and the College had won the Fforwm award for the development of bilingualism.

Coleg Llandrillo Cymru's continuing work in promoting the Welsh language and bilingualism was recognised by Fforwm when the College won the Development of Bilingualism Award.

The College continued to work collectively with the local education authorities and the schools to develop 14-19 learning pathways to widen choice. This included the delivery of the Vocational Futures programme for pre-16 learners, an expansion of the Rhyl College curriculum, a new Music Technology Centre in Denbigh and partnerships with the schools. Of particular note and a key feature of the WAG Transformation Policy was the

Michael Norton, Head of Finance, with responsibility for funding.

reorganisation of post-16 education in Rhyl and the creation of the Rhyl Sixth as part of the College development in Rhyl.

Enhanced Employer Engagement

Following the creation of the new Enterprise Directorate in 2005, (formerly the CSU), and the successful launch of Business Point in May 2006 at the ELWY Centre, the College witnessed unparalleled growth in employer engagement. With the successful acquisition of the former Bangor University work-based contract

and a 40% increased training contract, an increase in the number of courses and increasing attention to developing HE course progression, success was rewarded with Star Status within the Best Companies Accreditation standard for 2007. Llandrillo was one of only four colleges in the UK ever to have received this award.

By January 2008, the Enterprise Directorate had reached the pinnacle of success: the Estyn Inspection of Work Based Learning awarded the College straight grade ones across all areas. Not content with this accolade, the College went on to win the Beacon Award for 'College Engagement with Employers' in 2009.

Developing skills in key sector priority areas included Hospitality & Tourism, Health & Care, Engineering & Manufacturing, Built Environment and Retail & Business Services. In partnership with the SSCs, the College sought to establish, advance and maintain the education, skills and training of people employed in business and industry, including the public sector. By 2008/09, the College was working with

The Beacon award for College engagement with employers recognising the work provided by Business Point, the specialist business unit of the College is accepted by Derwena Watkin, Director of Enterprise.

14 sectors and over 300 employers drawn from across North Wales.

New state-of-the-art facilities for Marine Engineering and the Built Environment in 2009 and for Health & Care in 2010, together with dedicated facilities for Retail qualifications at the Rhyl College, provided an enhanced range of courses and training opportunities for businesses and employees.

Expanding Higher Education—was achieved primarily through Foundation degrees, working again in partnership with the SSCs and employers. Examples included the Foundation degree in Police Studies, developed in partnership with North Wales Police and the Foundation degree in Tourist Guiding developed as a solution to the lack of Blue Badge Guides in Wales. In total, eleven new Foundation degrees were developed and validated plus a BA (Hons) top-up in Deaf Studies, the first in Wales. The strategy included the appointment of a Director of Student Recruitment, stronger relationship marketing with school 6th forms and the delivery of a HE preparation module to level 3 learners.

Members of the Community Team with Sheila Jones who was responsible for widening participation (far right).

The presentation of a Beacon award for achieving excellence in supporting students in the College's international operations.

Widening Participation

This included an extension of rural developments, basic skills for migrant workers and overseas developments. The quality of provision across the counties of Denbighshire and Conwy was reviewed in November 2005 and February 2006 as a result of two Adult Community Inspections and once again the level of education and training was awarded 'excellence' – the best outcomes achieved at that time in Wales. The College developed and extended provision at two new centres: the Glasdir Learning Centre in Llanrwst delivering IT skills and qualifications and the Bay Learning Centre in Colwyn Bay.

There was also a further response to the Basic Skills agenda utilising the European funded Basic Skills Academy, Skills for Life mentors, and improved technology and blended approaches through e-learning.

The College expanded International/ Overseas provision by opening new markets in India, Nepal and Bangladesh and expanding A level opportunities in China. In 2008, the College appointed an International Development Manager to take the area forward. In 2009/10, the College won the Beacon Award for achieving excellence for International Student Support from recruitment to qualification. Around one hundred overseas students were recruited by the College and the College partners overseas, from Pakistan, China, Croatia, Morocco, India and Vietnam.

Another success for the College, this time for its outstanding efforts towards waste reduction.

Enhancing Customer Care

This included an upgrade to the College enquiry system, the introduction of on-line tracking systems to support work-based assessors track trainees' progress and improved attendance monitoring from the on-line register system.

Sustainable Development and Global Citizenship

This became an important feature of the College curriculum, which the College deemed essential not only for all its learners but also a necessary part in the review of its own practices in managing the College Estate. The newly developed College Environmental Action Plan focused on a set of targets concerning sustainable development which formed part of the Green Dragon Environmental Standard certification at level 4 and level 5. By 2008/09, demonstrating significant reductions in the use of gas and electricity, the College became the first multi-site College in Wales to achieve level 5, the highest of the Green Dragon awards. In 2010, the College won the Sustainability Award at the Wales Public Sector Waste

and Sustainability award ceremony for its outstanding efforts to reduce waste.

Learning Excellence

At the heart of the strategic vision lay a commitment to client accessibility, innovative learning and excellence. Following the Inspection of 2005, the College was able to demonstrate that students in the community, the workplace, the classroom and in the virtual world were all beneficiaries of a very responsive and excellent College.

The importance placed on outcomes and student attainment was an essential

College students beat off stiff competition from all the other colleges in Wales and England in the Welsh International Culinary Competition, held at the Rhos campus. Winning three of the top five team awards, the College also boasted the best results overall with College students winning over 50 awards.

part of the quality system. Using a wide range of techniques including teaching observations, focus groups, module and course evaluations and questionnaires, College management were able to identify strengths and areas for improvement. With over 20 Estyn trained Associate Assessors and Inspectors, lecturing, teaching and student support staff were observed annually to ensure that the quality of learning was the highest possible. The Student Perception of Programme (SPOP) survey was an anonymous biannual survey in which students evaluated College life and their experience of study. Delivered by impartial staff, the survey represented a rigorous collection of open and honest student opinion.

All aspects of satisfaction in 2006/07 scored above 90%, a position that continued throughout the remainder of the decade.

Julia Hughes (far right), Head of Coleg Llandrillo Cymru Denbigh, celebrates with two members of staff who won top awards at a NIACE Adult Tutor & Mentor Awards Ceremony in 2009/10.

Student satisfaction
92% were satisfied with their programme of study
90% enjoyed their course
93% would recommend the course to others
94% would encourage others to attend college

Success is also measured by performance and by 2009/2010, the key performance indicators were:

- Retention 91%, Attainment 89% and Successful Completion at 79% – all above national comparators;

- A level pass rates: 98.8% with 78.6% awarded grade A-C;

- International Baccalaureate: 95% achieved the full qualification;

- Welsh Baccalaureate 80% gained the Advanced Diploma and 81% gained the Intermediate Diploma;

- Access to HE: – 100% for Business, Law, Computing and Humanities & Science pathways.

An Enhanced Llandrillo Learning Network

After an exhilarating start to the millennium, the College continued its momentum with a series of developments that not only enhanced the curriculum portfolio but transformed post-16 educational provision across the Learning Network. In line with the strategic aim to increase and widen

participation, the College continued to report the highest participation rates in education and training in Wales at well above 10% of the local catchment area.

This is shown through a further extension to the Llandrillo Learning Network which highlights the scale of new building developments and the continued growth in the curriculum offer to students.

Coleg Llandrillo Rhyl

In 2005, the College successfully acquired the Rhyl Community College site and began to plan for an extension of the curriculum. The proposals received approval and

finance from the newly appointed DCELLS in 2006 and by 2007, following a £4.8 million refurbishment, Rhyl Community College was officially re-launched by the First Minister, Rt Hon Rhodri Morgan. The refurbishment included a transformation of the front elevations, a new two storey construction skills centre, a gas training centre, nail and hair salons and upgraded student support areas.

As a committed member of the 'Rhyl Going Forward' strategy – the framework adopted for the regeneration

The Rhyl College as it is today, including the Rhyl Sixth to the rear.

The newly elected First Minister, Mr Carwyn Jones, opens the Rhyl Sixth as part of Coleg Llandrillo Cymru Rhyl, an amalgamation of all post-16 education in the town.

of Rhyl under the Department of Work & Pensions City Strategy scheme launched in 2007 – the College started working together with its partners to develop a range of programmes and initiatives to provide additional support to help local people find and sustain employment.

The newly embedded Centre for Automotive Technology was also justifiably proud that year having gained a top five place in the Institute of Motor Industry's Centre of the Year award as well as seeing one of its students named as the IMI Student of the Year, beating almost 50,000 other students nationwide.

Celia Jones, Director of Coleg Llandrillo Cymru Rhyl.

Rhyl Sixth

By 2008, the College was engaged in the reorganisation of post-16 education in Rhyl. Set against the WAG 'Transformation' programme, the result was the closure of two school sixth forms and the creation of the Rhyl Sixth – an amalgamation of post-16 education provisions from the Rhyl College, Rhyl High School and Blessed Edward Jones High School. In 2010, Welsh Assembly approved and funded new buildings, to be constructed as an integral part of the existing campus at Rhyl College. This allowed the College to extend and enhance AS/A levels and vocational opportunities for young people to support the Rhyl regeneration programme.

Coleg Llandrillo Denbigh

Constantly battling to contain a growing number of students within the restrictions of the accommodation available, partnership working and flexibility became a major strength within Denbigh College. With the development of taster provision for the over-50s, new Return-to-Learn programmes and Basic Skills initiatives and flexibly delivered accountancy and finance programmes for businesses, the Denbigh College demonstrated its support for local and national needs.

In 2006/07, Denbigh Community College took on the joint responsibility of the adult centres at Ysgol Glan Clwyd and Denbigh High School opening an additional educational hub as part of the Glasdir Rural Development Centre in Llanrwst.

Glasdir Learning Centre

Glasdir is a rural development centre which serves the community of Llanrwst and the surrounding areas. In January 2007, the College agreed to support a bilingual community learning unit within the Centre with purpose-built training rooms, IT suites and conference facilities.

In 2007/08, the Centre successfully attracted funds from the European Agricultural Fund Rural Development programme to extend bilingual rural business development for a further 3 years.

Bilingual full-time courses included Access to Higher Education, Business Administration, Childcare and Health & Social Care. Part-time courses included Business, Computing & Accounting, Family History, GCSEs and Return-to-Learn programmes.

Coleg Llandrillo Abergele

Over several years, the Abergele College had developed an enhanced family history provision. In 2007/08, in recognition of their work, the Coleg Llandrillo Abergele

family history programme was named as an authorised branch and part of the research systems of the Genealogical Society of Utah, one of the largest in the world – the only branch in Wales and only the second in the UK to receive such an award.

Working closely with the then Conwy and Denbighshire NHS Trusts, the College ran medical courses with outstanding examination results and students securing employment with local hospitals.

In spring 2008, the Denbigh Community College launched its bilingual Music Technology Centre. Working closely with the high schools in Denbighshire, this provision opened its doors to students in September 2008.

Coleg Llandrillo Cymru Abergele
plays host to the Prime Minister,
Tony Blair and the Chancellor,
Gordon Brown in 2005; and
again to David Cameron, Prime
Minister in 2010.

Whilst never an intention, the Abergele
Community College has also become an
important venue for political leaders on
their campaign trail, reflecting the sensitive
political balance of the area. In April 2005,
the College welcomed Tony Blair and
Gordon Brown.

In 2010, the College played host to David
Cameron during his election campaign.

The Bay Learning Centre

The Bay Learning Centre opened
in Colwyn Bay in April 2010. It was
developed by Coleg Llandrillo Cymru in
partnership with Communities First and
the Youth Service, with support from the
Welsh Assembly Government and the Bay
Life Initiative, a total grant of £1.4 million.

The Centre offers a range of courses,
including Learn Direct, Classroom
Assistants, Deaf Studies and IT courses,
as well as courses to help people back
into learning. A custom-built Deaf Studies
suite provides dedicated facilities for Sign
Language and related courses.

The Bay Learning Centre,
Colwyn Bay.

The Elwy Centre

The Elwy Centre became the home of
Business Point in 2006 and assumed
responsibility for all College initiatives to
promote employer engagement. Set within
the newly developed Enterprise Directorate,
the operation has rapidly established itself
as one of the most successful of its kind
across the region.

The Rhos Campus

It is fair to say that the College's estates
strategies have always been ambitious.
Over the duration of twenty years,
seldom was there a break from building
developments at the Rhos campus. The
final years of our history record are no
exception, with staff being asked on
an annual basis for their patience and

perseverance as the developers remodelled and created new buildings to support the growth of the College. Building on the Rhos campus began again in earnest in 2007. From the entrance at the front to the sports pitch at the back, the works may best be described as a transformation. Using a complex mix of grant monies from the Welsh Assembly Government, support from the Strategic Regeneration Area fund and the College's own reserves, the Estates Strategy during 2006-2010 provided over £17 million of new buildings and infrastructure.

A pitch worth waiting for!

The Institute of Sport

For those who worked in the Sport & Recreation areas, two key developments, after years of promises, were particularly satisfying: the long overdue refurbishment of the Sports Centre at a cost of £1 million in 2007 and the completion of a third generation (3G) sports pitch at a cost of £750,000, leading to the launch of the Institute of Sport (Academi Llandrillo) in 2010. Aimed primarily at football and rugby, the Academi provided opportunities for talented athletes enabling them to play sport and study a wide range of curriculum including AS/A2 levels, business, sports

qualifications and more. The programmes are designed to give students their taught sessions in the morning leaving the afernoons free for physical, technical, tactical and psychological development under the guidance of professional coaches and sports scientists. The Academi also boasts strong links with the Welsh Rugby Union.

A year of sporting achievements with some of the students proudly displaying their Welsh caps for rugby and football. It was also a year when Mark Webster, student in Plumbing, was crowned Champion of the World at darts.

Marine and Built Environment Centre

Chris Smith, Director of Technology & Innovation (below) welcomes guests to the opening of the MBEC Centre.

Having successfully extended the Rhyl Community College and refurbished the Sports Centre during the summer of 2007, the College turned its attention to the final part of the Engineering Strategy, the Marine & Built Environment Centre (MBEC). With grant support from DCELLS, the £8.2 million Centre opened its doors to students in September 2009, offering state-of-the-art facilities for for the study of Construction, Marine Technology and Sustainability & Renewable Energy courses.

The Renewable Energy & Sustainability Centre for Wales (RESCW) formed part of the new MBEC and provided local communities, businesses, schools and individuals with facilities for demonstrations, educational visits and seminars, as well as installer training and Continuous Personal Development courses.

It is also fitting to record that this development looks out to the rapidly expanding wind farm development off the North Wales coast. The MBEC will play a significant part in supporting the training needs and developing skills appropriate for these new forms of sustainable power

The College says goodbye to the workshops as they pave the way for additional parking and a truly enhanced vista ... sadly, this pair of boots was never claimed by their owner before the bulldozers arrived!

which are increasingly required as Wales seeks other forms of sustainable energy.

The demolition of the old Engineering and Construction Workshops that had taken pride of place at the entrance to the Rhos campus should also be noted. With suitably new replacement buildings spread across the Learning Network, demolition paved the way for additional car parking and an enhanced panoramic view of the Golf Course – transformation indeed!

Dr Ian Rees, newly appointed Deputy Principal, Dr Roy Bichan, Vice Chair, Mary Burrows, Chief Executive of the Betsi Cadwaladr University Health Board and Maggie Griffiths, Director of Health and Care at the opening of the Institute of Health.

The new Institute of Health and Administrative block.

The Institute of Health

In September 2010, the £3.6 million Institute of Health & Social Care was completed, addressing the Continuing Professional Development (CPD) and vocational Higher Education needs of those working in the North Wales Health & Care Sector.

The new Institute, funded by WAG, included a ward area for teaching and training as well as a purpose-built counselling training suite, a lecture theatre, IT facilities and high specification classrooms. Training is undertaken by a qualified team of staff with tutors having clinical backgrounds e.g. in physiotherapy and nursing, along with extensive experience of teaching and training within the NHS and local authorities.

The curriculum which covers a wide range of staff, including carers, care assistants, health care assistants, support workers, clerical workers, porters, domestic workers and voluntary staff had been designed to facilitate accredited qualifications through bite-sized chunks of learning.

A New Administrative Block

Curriculum and students have always taken priority in the allocation of resources at Coleg Llandrillo Cymru and for many administrative staff, purpose-built accommodation was simply a dream. However, for the staff of 2009, this dream became a reality with a brand new block with panoramic views of the sea and the seagulls! Relocating from their base in the old, but extremely versatile hall, the newly vacated space paved the way for enhanced student and staff refreshment and relaxation facilities as part of the Heartspace development.

New Student/Staff Refreshment Areas

There has never been a space like the old hall. Having hosted the official opening of the College, been the set for College dances and events, been the College sports facility – not forgetting a major administration area, our history record concludes with a mixture of sadness and happiness. The old hall has most certainly gone, safe only in the memories of the staff who used it, but for the students and staff of the day it now has a new lease of life: an added floor and a brand new student and staff lounge area over two floors, located in the heart of the college.

The new student lounge area.

Coleg Llandrillo Cymru and Coleg Meirion Dwyfor
merge to create an enhanced Coleg Llandrillo Cymru.

Merger with Coleg Meirion-Dwyfor

Dr Ian Rees, former Principal of Coleg Meirion Dwyfor, Huw Evans OBE, Lord Dafydd Elis Thomas, Honorary President of Coleg Llandrillo Cymru, and John Bellis celebrate the merger in Cardiff Bay.

We conclude this history record with the merger of Coleg Meirion-Dwyfor and Coleg Llandrillo Cymru which undoubtedly has created a new and stronger institution serving Dwyfor, Meirionnydd, Conwy and Denbighshire and the surrounding areas. With a critical mass which will influence the shape and development of colleges elsewhere in Wales, the merger will set the standard for other mergers in the future.

The process started in March 2008 when the Coleg Meirion-Dwyfor Corporation identified the need to seek a formal partnership with another institution. Following initial exploratory discussions with two potential partners, the Corporation decided to proceed with Coleg Llandrillo Cymru. By July 2009, both Boards had agreed to move to the detailed planning and consultation stage and by December 2009 detailed proposals were submitted to the Welsh Assembly Government for approval. This was granted on 1st April 2010. The official launch of the extension of Coleg Llandrillo Cymru followed later that month at the Senedd's Pierhead building, Cardiff Bay.

The merger has brought together 1,400 staff and 24,000 learners with a budget of £46 million. This will support Coleg Meirion-Dwyfor to secure and further develop post-16 education and training opportunities in the area, including opportunities for local businesses, and enable Coleg Llandrillo Cymru to further enhance learner opportunities and the bilingual nature of the Institution.

As part of the revised governance arrangements, five new Board members were appointed and the new Board of Coleg Llandrillo Cymru was charged with taking the College forward to providing the highest quality education and training across North West Wales, whilst preserving localised specialisms. The new planning framework has meant additional courses at the Coleg Meirion-Dwyfor campuses and established clear progression pathways through the newly enhanced network.

It is therefore no surprise to record that following this successful merger with Coleg Meirion-Dwyfor, the newly extended Coleg Llandrillo Cymru is still proud to report that performance indicators within the quality profile remain well above the national average.

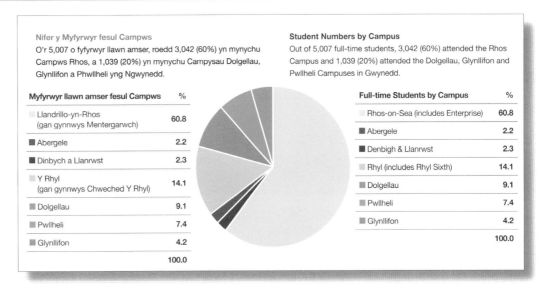

Nifer y Myfyrwyr fesul Campws

O'r 5,007 o fyfyrwyr llawn amser, roedd 3,042 (60%) yn mynychu Campws Rhos, a 1,039 (20%) yn mynychu Campysau Dolgellau, Glynllifon a Phwllheli yng Ngwynedd.

Myfyrwyr llawn amser fesul Campws	%
Llandrillo-yn-Rhos (gan gynnwys Mentergarwch)	60.8
Abergele	2.2
Dinbych a Llanrwst	2.3
Y Rhyl (gan gynnwys Chweched Y Rhyl)	14.1
Dolgellau	9.1
Pwllheli	7.4
Glynllifon	4.2
	100.0

Student Numbers by Campus

Out of 5,007 full-time students, 3,042 (60%) attended the Rhos Campus and 1,039 (20%) attended the Dolgellau, Glynllifon and Pwllheli Campuses in Gwynedd.

Full-time Students by Campus	%
Rhos-on-Sea (includes Enterprise)	60.8
Abergele	2.2
Denbigh & Llanrwst	2.3
Rhyl (includes Rhyl Sixth)	14.1
Dolgellau	9.1
Pwllheli	7.4
Glynllifon	4.2
	100.0

	2005/06	2009/10	NC
Retention	87%	91%	90%
Attainment	83%	89%	85%
Successful Completion	67%	79%	76%

Student numbers taken from the Annual Report 2009/10.

So, as the millennium came to a close, student numbers at the newly merged College rose to over 24,600 spanning three counties and some ten campuses, with a quality profile well above the national average. A job well done for an Institution that started with only a handful of adult education classes in 1905!

Memberts of the new College Board (left to right):
Cllr John Bellis, Helen Halpin, Glyn Catley, Cllr Dewi Owens,
Jane Howells, Dr John Llewellyn, Bethan Roberts, Peter Lavin,
Cllr Dewi Lewis, Dr Roy Bichan, Huw Jones, Chris Jackson, OBE,
David Hicken, Huw Evans, OBE, Hedd Pugh, Alun Thomas
Inset: David Williams, Dr Anne Hynes, Cllr Wyn Jones, Geraint Hughes

Bu'n fraint cofnodi hanes a llwyddiant Coleg Llandrillo Cymru am ei fod yn stori go iawn o arwain drwy weledigaeth, strategaeth wedi'i diffinio'n glir, brwdfrydedd, ymrwymiad a balchder. Ers cychwyn digon gwylaidd ym 1905 mae Coleg Llandrillo Cymru bellach wedi sefydlu ei hun fel un o'r prif sefydliadau yn y Deyrnas Unedig.

Mae cyfraniad staff a myfyrwyr bob amser wedi bod yn ganmoladwy ac mae'n stori o lwyddiant sy'n parhau gyda'r traddodiad sy'n cael ei adlewyrchu yng nghyrhaeddiad myfyrwyr flwyddyn ar ôl blwyddyn. Prin iawn yw sefydliad yng Ngogledd Cymru – cwmnïau mawr, cwmnïau bach, y sector breifat neu gyhoeddus – sydd ddim yn cyflogi cyn-fyfyriwr o Goleg Llandrillo mewn rhyw gymhwysedd neu'i gilydd; ac mae hynny'n brawf ynddo'i hun o lwyddiant y sefydliad.

Ac felly i gloi mae'n bleser mawr gennyf longyfarch a dymuno'r gorau i'r Coleg wrth iddo symud ymlaen i'r cyfnod nesaf o'i ddatblygiad.

It has been a delight to place on record the history of and the success achieved by Coleg Llandrillo Cymru, simply because it is most genuinely a story of visionary leadership, a clearly defined strategy, enthusiasm, commitment and pride. From those humble beginnings in 1905, Coleg Llandrillo Cymru is now firmly established as one of the leading institutions in the UK.

The contribution of staff and students has been exemplary at all times and it is a success story that just keeps on going. This legacy is reflected year-on-year in student success. There is hardly an organisation in North Wales – large companies, small companies, private or public sector – that does not have a former Llandrillo College student employed in some capacity. Testimony in itself.

So it is with great pleasure that I conclude this College history, with congratulations and best wishes for the College as it begins to chart its next chapter of development.

APL—Accredited Prior Learning
ATTI—Association of Teachers in Technical Institutions
AVCE—Advanced Vocational Certificate of Education
BEC—Business Education Council
BTEC—Business & Technology Council
CAD/CAM—Computer Aided Design/Manufacturing
CARS—Community Auto's in Rhyl Project
CAT—Centre for Automotive Technology
CBETCC—Colwyn Bay Evening Technical Classes Committee
CCET—Community Consortium for Education and Training
CELTEC—The Learning & Skills Council for North Wales
CETW—Council for Education and Training in Wales
CGLI—City & Guilds of London Institute
CHWEAN—Coleg Harlech Workers Education Authority (North)
CIF—Common Investment Funding
CITB—Construction Industrial Training Board
CMIS—Computerised Management Information System
COTICC—Certificate of Tourist Information Competence Course
COVE—Centre of Vocational Excellence
CPD—Continuing Professional Development
CPVE—Certificate of Pre-Vocational Education
CREDIS—Welsh Credit Framework
CSE—Certificate of Secondary Education
CSU—Commercial Support Unit
CUNW—Community University of North Wales
CWLWM—Name for Conwy CCET
DARA—Defence Aviation Repair Agency
DCELLS—Department for Children, Education, Lifelong Learning & Skills
DLE—Demand Led Element
DTI—Department of Trade & Industry
EAB—Education Assets Board
ECDL—European Computer Driving Licence
EEC—European Economic Community
EFL—English as a Foreign Language
EITB—Engineering Industrial Training Board
ELWa—Education Learning Wales
ERA—Education Reform Act 1988
ERDF—European Regional Development Fund

ES—Employment Service
ESF—European Social Fund
ESTYN—The Inspectorate in Wales (HMI)
FE—Further Education
FEFCW—Further Education Funding Council for Wales
FFORWM—The Association of Welsh Colleges
FHE Act—Further & Higher Education Act
FTE—Full-time Equivalents
FTET—Full-time Education and Training
GCE—General Certificate of Education
GIF—Growth Incentive Fund
GNVQ—General National Vocational Qualifications
GWINTO—Gas and Water National Training Organisation
HCI—Hotel & Catering Institute
HE—Higher Education
HEFCW—Higher Education Funding Council for Wales
HNC—Higher National Certificate
HND—Higher National Diploma
IB—International Baccalaureate
ICT—Information Communication Technology
IDO—Integrated Development Operation
ILT—Information & Learning Technology
IMI—Institute of Motor Industry
INSET—In-Service Training
JANET—Joint Academic Network for Education & Training
KEF—Knowledge Exploitation Fund
LEA—Local Education Authority
LEATGS—Local Education Authorities' Training Grants
LEC—Local Employer Councils
MBEC—Marine & Built Environment Centre
MLE—Managed Learning Environment
MOF—Ministry of Food
MSC—Manpower Services Commission
NCETW—National Council for Education & Training for Wales
NCVQ—National Council for Vocational Qualifications
NEDS—National Economic Development Strategy
NETBWS—College Mobile IT Training facility
NEWI—North East Wales Institute
NEWTEC—North East Wales Training and Enterprise Council

NOF—National Opportunities Fund
NTET—National Targets for Education & Training
NTI—National Training Initiative
NVQ—National Vocational Qualification
NWAC—North Wales Access Consortium
NWYTA—North Wales Youth Training Agency, latterly **NWT**
OCN—Open College Network
ONC—Ordinary National Certificate
OND—Ordinary National Diploma
PGCE—Postgraduate Certificate in Education
POP—Peripatetic Outreach Programme
RESCW—Renewable Energy & Sustainability Centre for Wales
ROSLA—Raising of the School Leaving Age
RSA—Royal Society for the Arts
RTITB—Road Transport Industrial Training Board
SET—Selective Employment Tax
SFTE—Space Full-Time Equivalents
SME—Small and medium-sized enterprises
SPOP—Student Perception of Programme
SSC—Sector Skills Councils
TARGED—North West Wales TEC
TEC—Technician Education Council
TOP—Training Opportunities Programme
TPS—Teachers Pension Scheme
TQM—Total Quality Management
TRIST—TVEI-related In-Service Training
TVEI—Technical & Vocational Education Initiative
TVEI/E—Technical & Vocational Education Initiative/ Extension Project
UFI—University for Industry
UKERNA—United Kingdom Education and Research Networking Association
VLC—Virtual Learning Centre
VLE—Virtual Learning Environment
WAG—Welsh Assembly Government
WJEC—Welsh Joint Education Committee
WRNAFE—Work-related Non-Advanced Further Education
WVN—Welsh Video Network
YOP—Youth Opportunities Programme
YTS—Youth Training Scheme